A BLESSING IS IN IT

A BLESSING IS IN IT

How God Led an Alcoholic, *Fame-Seeking* Songwriter into *Nursing Home* Music Ministry

SUSAN PIPER

ONE KING
PRESS

Although the conversations recounted in this book are recreated from the author's actual memories of them, they do not necessarily represent word-for-word transcripts; space and time have, on occasion, been rearranged to suit the telling. To maintain anonymity, names and identifying factors have been changed.

© 2024 by Susan J. Piper

All rights reserved. No part of this publication may be reproduced without the prior written permission of the publisher, except in the case of brief quotations embodied in critical reviews and certain other noncommercial uses permitted by copyright law. For permission requests, contact the publisher at the address below.

One King Press | 307 N. Oak Street | Lititz, PA 17543 | www.onekingpress.com

Printed in the United States of America

Unless otherwise indicated, Scriptures quotations are taken from *The Holy Bible: King James Version*.
Scriptures marked NKJV are taken from the *New King James Version®*, Copyright © 1982 by Thomas Nelson, Inc. Used by permission. All rights reserved.
Scripture quotations marked ESV are from the *ESV® Bible (The Holy Bible, English Standard Version®)*, Copyright © 2001 by Crossway, a publishing ministry of Good News Publishers. Used by permission. All rights reserved.
Scriptures marked NLT are taken from the *Holy Bible, New Living Translation*, Copyright © 1996, 2004, 2007 by Tyndale House Foundation. Used by permission of Tyndale House Publishers, Inc., Carol Stream, Illinois 60188. All rights reserved.
Scriptures marked NIV are taken from *The Holy Bible, New International Version ®*, Copyright © 1973, 1978, 1984, 2011 by Biblica, Inc.™ Used by permission of Zondervan.

A Blessing Is in It | Susan J. Piper

Library of Congress Control Number: 2024946517

ISBN 979-8-9865464-2-1 Print
ISBN 979-8-9865464-3-8 eBook

Interior photographs courtesy of the author's private collection
Photograph of the author and Levi: © Gary Livingston
Cover and frontispiece design by Hannah Linder Designs

1 3 5 7 9 10 8 6 4 2

Dedication

To those who are so kind to say that I am their friend, who've convinced me I should write and sing and have led me to what is good and true: this book is for you.

And to those who were so deceived that they believed the lies they taught me, who drove me to the tears that brought me to myself and my God: this book is also for you.

Table of Contents

A Note to the Reader	IX
1. He Leadeth Me	1
2. Being Number One	6
3. Chloe	14
4. Jesus on the Main Line	19
5. Perfect	23
6. Too Much God	30
7. Love-Hate Relationship	34
8. Changes	38
9. You Can Do It	43
10. Motherhood	49
11. Martha and Me	54
12. My Father	59
13. Come In	65
14. Natural Causes	70
15. A Song	75

16.	Dear David	78
17.	My Little Town	85
18.	Get Well Soon	91
19.	Lunch	100
20.	God Will Take Care of You	103
21.	Mother's Day	108
22.	From Faith to Faith	112
23.	Tribute	117
24.	Rewriting History	122
25.	Carsick	126
26.	Dry Your Eyes	132
27.	The Conditions of Love	135
28.	Heaven	139
29.	Memorials	143
30.	John Prine	148
31.	Wishy-Washy	152
32.	Levi	156
33.	The Judgment	162
34.	Second-Chance Roses	168
35.	Wine	172
36.	Oil	176

37. Whom Have I?	182
38. This Little Light of Mine	187
39. Death and Life	191
40. Nice Things	198
41. Truth	205
42. People Get Ready	210
Parting Thoughts	216
Acknowledgments	218
About the Author	220

A Note to the Reader

I've always had a love for words. Even my teen-aged songwriting was word-driven. There's a safety in songwriting. You can hide your meaning, especially if you're poetic and good at melody. But in a book, you have to spell things out. There's no hiding. That's a very vulnerable place to be.

Risky as it was, I wanted to tell my story. And so I wrote my chapters. But when the editing process began, I discovered I hadn't told it at all. My editor repeatedly encouraged me to say what I was convinced I had already said. Turns out, I was still hiding.

Before I came to Christ, I had spent 15 years in therapy, working hard to understand the psychological abuse of my childhood and its impact on my life. But now I had to dig even deeper. I had to examine my demons under a microscope to effectively describe them to someone else. To you.

The Lord gave me a great blessing in this process. He held the hand of the little girl that I once was and together we looked at everything He wanted me to see. I am not the same person as when this project began. I seem to have grown up.

The other day I was astonished to find myself considering dedicating this book to my deceased parents. I soon realized it was because I'd forgiven them.

You may not have had the luxury of fifteen years of therapy (out of pocket, mind you). But whether you struggle to understand your feelings on a daily basis, or have never needed an hour of counsel in your life, I pray that you will find your own blessing in these pages. That you will meet yourself here. And most importantly, meet the Savior who rises with healing in His wings.

Susan Piper

*But for you who fear my name,
the Sun of Righteousness will rise with healing in his wings.
And you will go free,
leaping with joy like calves let out to pasture.*
Malachi 4:2 NLT

1

He Leadeth Me

The desert shall rejoice, and blossom as the rose.
Isaiah 35:1

Welcome to somewhere in the middle of a very forgettable period of my life.

At this point, I was still married to husband number two (he was not fond of that title) and had handed him the reins of my existence. Whatever fragments of my personality I had been able to piece together so far were rapidly disappearing.

At the same time, my twenty-year attempt to succeed as a songwriter had left me with nothing new to say and no desire to say it. With no songs in me to write and no gigs to play, I was reduced to working in the gift shop around the corner which sold the odd combination of handmade jewelry and fireplace supplies. It was located beside what folks used to call the "old age home."

One day the bell over the door sounded, announcing a dear and floundering soul in a heavy wig. You could tell she was lost and had most likely escaped from next door. I didn't even hesitate. "May I walk you home?"

I obtained her permission, gave her my arm, and out we went.

It was a short walk, but every step was full of meaning. Suddenly I had the unfamiliar sense that I was doing something worthwhile. I felt the faintest hint of what must have been hope. Even if I couldn't write songs, surely the world would have more than one option to offer someone like me. I had to try to find it before I withered away in retail. The gift shop was so incredibly dull.

Looking in the classifieds that night, I found only one ad that matched my limited skill set. "Creative and musical abilities a plus," it said. An entry-level position was available in the activities department of an assisted living residence.

Walking into the facility, my deadened senses came alive. I fell in love with every fragile creature I saw. If the position hadn't boasted the whopping pay rate of six dollars an hour, I would have been tempted to work for free.

Instead, at the conclusion of my suspiciously brief interview, the administrator folded her hands and beamed at me.

"We'd like to hire you as our new activities director."

How could this be? I had attended only three years of high school, as I had been very busy coming apart at the seams. Although I graduated on a technicality, I certainly had gained no academic knowledge. Whatever had been impressed upon my psyche to that point would have been of no service in a professional capacity. But for no earthly reason, I had gotten the job.

Looking back, I think they wanted me to fill the position until they could hire a "real" director. No one was more surprised than I that everything so wonderfully clicked.

I was creative! We had a Jello eating contest involving the residents, the local grade school, trays of wiggly stuff, and lots of bibs. Once I brought in sand for a day at the beach where everyone wore their bathrobes and played balloon volleyball. (I know a director who brought in a pony. I never went that far.)

Once a week I led a sing-along for the residents. If someone was too ill to attend, I would stop by their room and sit on their bed and sing to them. This was nothing like entertainment, ponies, or volleyball. This was a personal exchange.

Since I was a new (and unqualified) boss, I was given an assistant. Ron was easily more professional than I and incredibly sweet to work with. A temporarily retired minister, he drove the bus for our outings.

Ron prayed about everything. He introduced me to a God who seemed to care about it all. Nothing was too small or not church-y enough for his Heavenly Father. He didn't "lead me to the Lord," as people say, but when he prayed for me, I felt I was being brought by the hand to God.

For five years I remained a salaried employee with a title and health insurance. That came in handy during my second divorce.

Then came a new administrator with a new agenda—which was not in my original job description. This woman wasn't satisfied with a good performance from her employees. She expected adoration, and I wasn't prepared to bow down.

"Susan, I wish you could see the expression on your face," Ron said, shaking his head at me. He was only trying to help me out. I didn't like our new commander and my face was a tale bearer. But still, I thought if I just did my job and kept to myself and the residents, I would be fine.

I wasn't fine. I got fired.

Ron wasn't working that day. When I called him at his home, crying, he prayed for me right over the phone. Later he showed up at my door with a cake and a card of congratulations. Turns out he wasn't crazy about the politics at the facility either.

I loved my job and the people at that residence. My first night after being fired and sent away was very long and tearful. For the "protection" of the residents, they had hustled me out the back door with an escort like I was some kind of criminal. I didn't even get to say goodbye.

The next morning, I awoke with a fledgling plan. It would involve cold calling, which was not yet on my emergent list of character strengths. But it had to be done.

I called nursing home after nursing home with my just-born idea of "music visits." I explained I would go door-to-door and visit and sing, sitting with people and entering into their lives like a friend. Even though I was still years away from encountering the Lord Jesus, by the time unemployment ran out, I had a network of nursing homes and the beginning, the tiny little seedling, of a ministry yet to come.

In order to stay in touch with Ron, I joined his Bible study, with all my misconceptions of "religion" intact. There, I met the authentic Christians who would become my dearest friends before and especially after I was translated into the Kingdom alongside them.

From this first nursing home encounter, God used older adults to bring healing to my injured heart. At the facility, I was everyone's daughter. I was loved by fifty sets of parents who wanted nothing in return. Affection was safe, without the sexual snares I'd encountered in my past.

So many of the residents had lost so much—children, spouses, finances, homes. Yet they were able to look beyond themselves, and being with them helped me do the same. My years of therapy had been necessary, as you will soon understand. But you can only look inside for so long, and I was in danger of becoming an expert on the dark, intramural workings of my subconscious. These dear people were taking my mind off me. And they still do that and more, every day.

I visit them, but they open their hearts to me. I ask them about their lives, and they tell me their stories. Sometimes it's the same story again and again, but it is so important it bears retelling. I knock, and they are glad to see me. I offer myself as a stranger, and they welcome me in without question. If the hymn is worthy of tears, they cry; it was their mother's favorite, it was played at their daughter's funeral. They don't or can't hide their feelings; they are who they are. They follow me down the hall. They say they were sad before I came and please come again because I've made their day. They have done more than that for me.

They've changed my life.

> *But God hath chosen the foolish things of the world*
> *to confound the wise;*
> *and God hath chosen the weak things of the world*
> *to confound the things which are mighty....*
> 1 Corinthians 1:27

2
Being Number One

This is not the pretty part, but I will not leave you here.

I grew up sitting at my mother's feet. That was not a good place to be. She used her children. Then again, she was ill; she's not here to defend herself. I was the youngest and the only girl, and I believe the most pressure fell on me. Maybe my brothers would disagree.

Night after night I would follow her into the living room where she sat in the dark with her wine. She never turned on a light. It was my job to listen to her cry.

No one else loved her, she said. My father didn't love her, my brothers didn't need her. It was only me, she said, and I was number one. I was the reason she was staying in our house. If it weren't for me, she would leave. All her sad secrets were only for me. When the evening's session had ended, I was to walk out with a cheerful expression on my face and pretend I hadn't heard a thing. I followed my mother's lead.

Looking good was the most important thing to my mother. Instead of a baby, she wanted a perfect little doll. Once I could talk, I was to be a perfect little lady. She had signals for the dinner-time performance. Clearing her throat if I was too loud or too demanding. Tapping my leg under the table if I'd said something wrong.

I remember the blue poofy dress I wore to perform for her bridge club when I was about four. I sang and attempted to dance for them just like Shirley Temple. (The ballet lessons hadn't helped;

Shirley was the daughter my mother really wanted.) In kindergarten, for show and tell, I stood up and sang a rousing version of "Goody, Goody" that my mother had personally taught me:

> *So you met someone who set you back on your heels,*
> *Goody, Goody!*
> *So you met someone and now you know how it feels,*
> *Goody Goody!*
> *Hooray and hallelujah, you had it comin' to ya,*
> *Goody good for her...goody goody for you...*
> *And I hope you're satisfied, you rascal you!*[1]

Revenge for a broken heart was my poor mother's theme. For years it was mine, too.

By the time I'd arrived at kindergarten, I knew that getting a boyfriend was a top priority. That's what made you valuable. I had a list of little hopefuls, all rated and numbered in order of preference. I was a smart little girl.

I had an image to build and maintain as well. By fifth grade I wore a padded bra and fishnet stockings held up by a garter belt. My mother instructed me in walking with a book on my head, holding my stomach in. Boys didn't like fat little girls, either.

Through it all, no matter how I was treated, I was to respond with self-denial. "You be the big one," my mother insisted. Never mind that I was so young and deserved to be defended—and had feelings of my own.

Being number one didn't endear me to my brothers. For some reason, during a particularly horrid trailer-trip vacation in which my father spanked my mother in front of us (don't ever put a

---

1. Lyrics © 1936 Johnny Mercer

dysfunctional family into a small trailer and expect to have fun), I was overcome by an urge to tell my brothers that my mother had told me I was her favorite. I have no idea why, or if I even knew how cruel I was being. I just remember one brother blurting out "She didn't say that!" *Oh, I am so sorry. Can you ever forgive me?* In later years, my other brother confided (loudly) to me, "I hated you growing up." *I know. I don't blame you at all.*

As I got older, I attempted to keep my number-one position, but I sensed that I was losing ground. Needs of my own were pushing in and would soon refuse to be silenced. I was entering junior high school.

The girls had a gym teacher we all loved. Ms. Rolin (not her real name) was young, and being close to us in age increased her appeal. She joked with all the girls, treating us more like peers than students, but I was teacher's pet. By now you know I had to be.

But the amazing thing was she seemed to really like *me*. She didn't ask for anything from me. She was always so glad to see me. She even gave me a nickname: "Hello, Sunshine!" Something new was happening—I think it was the first time I'd ever loved anyone. Without realizing it, I was pulling away from my mother. I adored my teacher.

But Ms. Rolin was not appropriate with the girls in her classes. She would take us in her car to her apartment. I had my first drink there. She did not molest me, or anyone, to my knowledge. Unlike the minister at our respectable church. Unlike the twenty-three-year-old "manager" I had when I was fifteen who would pick me up in his sports car to take me to his home for "rehearsal." Ms. Rolin was not appropriate, but she didn't harm me. However, she was a woman, and that was enough to threaten my mother. She let the sports car take me away, but she didn't like Ms. Rolin.

In retrospect, Ms. Rolin was most likely a lesbian. Or at least a very loose thinker. Those were the days when such things were still shameful, and as a Christian now, I know God's good purpose in giving us shame for our sins. Godly sorrow leads us to repentance, and God cleanses and forgives. I know this firsthand, and I pray you do, too. He doesn't give us shame to torment us. He's the cure.

But my mother had the times on her side. Do you hear my old bitterness? The fact is, since I agree with God, I must partly agree with my mother, at least regarding right and wrong. But as to her motives and methods—ah, that's the tricky part.

At the end of my junior high term, Ms. Rolin was going back to college for the summer, and I was graduating. I didn't know if I'd see her again. She gave me her gym whistle and ring and promised to write. I kept her letters with my treasures and my diary in a tin in the bottom of my dresser drawer, hidden safely away.

Meanwhile, my mother worked as a hall monitor in the high school where I'd attend the next fall, where the school board met. She knew people.

One day she stood in the doorway of my bedroom. Her stance was one of great victory. Her words were cold as ice.

"I found your whistle and ring and letters and diary and took them to the school board and had her fired. Ms. Rolin won't be coming back." She had taken my dearest friend away and exposed my secrets to everyone. I was ruined.

I didn't need therapy to tell me my mother had done that for herself, not for me. I knew right then who she really cared about. She was threatened by this woman, and she would not be beaten, even if she had to crush me to keep me. So much for being number one.

I entered high school with great shame. Not shame for my sins, not some surface shame that would slough off my shoulders as I grew, but a shame that became an integral part of my being. I had been teacher's pet to an accused lesbian and had gotten her fired. I had seen through my mother. I was all alone.

Soon I began bouncing off the walls. (Turns out no amount of my mother's tapping me under the table could make me into a quiet person.) At home, I locked myself in my bedroom with my guitar, desperately writing songs to silence the demons of emotion that had become my tormentors. I was screaming for help, and I did most of it during school hours. I had my first anxiety attack in the office with the school counselor, whom I also adored. *Oh, please take care of me.* He suggested family therapy with my parents. Flashback to the vacation in the trailer.

The psychologist at the clinic said he'd never heard the word "hate" bandied about so much at a family therapy session before.

We met only three times. The last time (and I don't remember what prompted her question), my mother asked me, "Sue,"—*Don't you ever call me that. My name is Susan*—"Sue, would you be happier if I were dead?"

I had an answer. But I couldn't say it. I don't even want to write it down now. I stood up and screamed and ran out of the room and down the long hall. We were up on a high floor of the clinic. At the end of the hall was a floor-to-ceiling window. Looking back, I'm sure it was safety glass, so I may never have made it through, but I recall how the possibility flashed through my mind. Next to the window was a door to the fire escape. I crumpled in a heap on the top stair. I heard all the footsteps coming after me.

The good doctor invited me back to his office alone. Then he invited me into the hospital for a few weeks. He was interested in saving my life. I said yes immediately. To get out of that house, I would have even gone to prison. He probably saved me from that, too.

My mother counseled me. "You have problems, Sue, this will make you stronger." *(It's Susan...)* "And you should thank your father for spending all this money."

I loved the hospital. I hated going home on weekends, but I loved the hospital. I had no restrictions; I could go through any locked doors because everyone knew I had no intention of leaving. The nurses said I was a "refreshing patient." The anxiety attacks went away. I went to arts and crafts and made a cross out of copper. I still wonder what happened to that.

So, you start high school full of shame and notoriety and then you spend a few weeks in the psychiatric ward; chances are good you will not be going to the prom.

But even as a teenager the downtown bars embraced me and my guitar, men always welcomed me, alcohol killed the pain, and I was going to be a star. Thank God that never happened or I probably wouldn't be writing to you now.

Before I knew it, I was almost eighteen and received permission to go to New Jersey to sing with a band. I skipped graduation and spent my eighteenth birthday trying out seven or eight different kinds of shots while sitting proudly at the bar. Sorry, I don't remember anything else about that party.

I married immediately, literally the first man I met on a bench outside the bar. I didn't know him, or myself. The band, thrown together for the sake of a Jersey Shore vacation, was fired before the summer's end. My new "bench-man" husband whisked me away to his apartment in Pennsylvania, where I began writing happy letters home. I "forgot" everything that happened there. I restored the family illusion from top to bottom. I was trained to do it, and my mother, the "real" illusionist, responded in kind. Everything was fine—everything but me.

Not surprisingly, my life wasn't working very well. I kept looking for a man to fix it for me, but I would always track down the one who would end up treating me like dirt. After two divorces, I was still a bloodhound for losers. I couldn't believe anyone could love me. I desperately wanted someone to, but I couldn't tolerate anyone who was even nice to me. This was a predicament. Pretty soon, I was once again having trouble working, sleeping, and breathing.

My first therapist as an adult tore down all my protective walls, showed me how false my perceptions were, and exposed the truth of my family situation. He didn't last long. I couldn't bear it and fired him and his reality.

My second therapist was the one who helped me. He went very slowly. He let me take down the walls myself, brick by brick. It took such a long time. But he was patient.

And he succeeded. I finally learned to face the truth without running from it. Maybe like an immunization: a little bit of sickness, then a little bit more, then the next thing you know, fifteen years later, you're not crying anymore.

But it was the Lord who gave me protection from my mother. He gave me a desire to move towards her, but permission to not invest my heart. It wasn't easy; it was a fine line to walk. He was teaching me about emotional boundaries. For His sake and mine I really did love her. But I didn't have to let her run me over like a train.

I remember exactly which apartment I was living in and where I was standing when we had the phone conversation during which she announced: "So and So is not number one any more, it's So and So now." She had changed the ratings between my brothers. I wonder if she ever told them, or if that information, too, was only for me.

For a long time, I asked the Lord what it was about her...what was wrong? I had read about borderline personality disorder before. But one day I came across an article from *Psychology Today* written from the perspective of being raised by a parent with the illness. There I met my childhood. There I found my answer.

How I wish I could tell you now that our relationship had been healed and restored before she died. I tried. But she wasn't open to discussion: she never did anything wrong, the old cases were all closed and the locks were rusted shut. I did share about Christ with her, again and again. I never saw enough sincerity to know what she really believed.

Until the end, my mother was in charge of even our phone calls, determining the length and the hang-up point; she was always in charge of everything. But there is a day that no one can control. There is no discharge from that war. I saw her a few weeks before she died.

I had visited from Pennsylvania and brought my guitar into the nursing home. By then my mother was barely able to speak, but as I sang an old hymn she joined in. She had a beautiful voice; she had taught me to harmonize when I was a little girl.

I went back in the morning to see her briefly before returning home. As I stood up to say goodbye, a sudden "NO!" leaped from deep inside of her. I went back to hold her. I cried. I'm crying now, telling you. No, there were no reconciling words between us, but God gave us a moment.

And in spite of everything, I'd have to say that was love.

And be ye kind one to another,
tenderhearted, forgiving one another,
even as God for Christ's sake hath forgiven you.
Ephesians 4:32

3

Chloe

I found my first dog at the S.P.C.A.

She was being returned by a woman who said her two-year-old daughter was afraid of her. That should have given me pause. But the dog was named "Piper," and I thought it was a cue from the Cosmos, or some kind of Synchronicity. So, I adopted her. I did change her name to Murphy. "Piper Piper" was just too odd.

Murphy was a scruffy, scrappy, terrier mix. Very smart, though not smart enough to not snap and snarl at her owner. We eventually reached an understanding. Since it would still be eight years until I would come to Christ, I wouldn't have respected a dog that was tender and mild anyway. I was pretty snarly myself.

Poor Murphy didn't change much over the years. After my conversion, as my church was moving me into a new apartment, I imprisoned her in the bathroom with a big warning sign that read CAREFUL: MURPHY INSIDE! Enough said.

When she died at age sixteen it was very sad of course. I had loved her as best I could. She was company. But now I was coming home to an empty apartment and it was hard. My prayer group of ladies decided to pray for a new dog for me. I wasn't sure I was ready, but they were.

The leader, a missionary friend, prayed that:
1: God would pick the perfect dog for me
2: A mature dog, not a puppy

3: A dog someone was looking to find a home for
4: Free (a sure sign of a missionary prayer)

I didn't say a word. I was thinking I'd like a girl and thought two years old would be perfect, but I didn't even pray, I just thought it. My friends took over.

Two weeks later, pulling into the parking lot of one of my nursing homes, a car passed me with its window cavity consumed by the smiling face of the most adorable dog I'd ever seen. A hound nose, scruffy fur, big eyes, long ears flapping in the wind. I jumped out and approached the owner, who was releasing her four-legged charmer from the back seat.

"Excuse me, what kind of dog is that?"

"A PBGV."

"A what?"

"Petit Basset Griffon Vendeen. It means small, low, rough coated, from Vendeen, France." She was used to such questions.

I was smitten. "How much do they run?"

"A dog like this, a show dog? As much as two thousand."

"Oh! Well, that's out of my range," I said, my hopes falling.

"You could get a pet for maybe eight hundred."

"Um...still out of my range."

"Sometimes people are looking to find a home for their dog...."
(See above prayer list.)

"Oh, you could sign me up for that," I said, my hopes rising.

"Really, like maybe an older dog?"
(See above prayer list!)

She reached into her purse for a pen and jotted down a contact name and number. She even hugged me. How often do strangers do such things? When I finished my nursing home hour, I raced to my car to send out an emergency prayer APB: "*Pray* for a PBGV! Wait till you see this dog! I think God is answering our prayers!"

I went online to learn about the breed and was reminded of how expensive they were. Even a rescue required a hefty adoption fee. I called the number I'd been given, and the woman who answered had one PBGV she was selling for five hundred dollars. A bargain, maybe, but certainly not free.

As I considered it, my resolve weakened and I wondered if maybe this was the answer to our prayer after all. Maybe God was just skipping a few specifications. A few days later I called back but that dog was no longer available. My contact gave me two more names and numbers of breeders to try. I was artless enough to tell her I was hoping the dog would be free. Before we hung up, she reminded me: "People don't give away dogs like this."

I did some online research on the kennels. Kennel number one was owned by a couple who were living together and not married, so I chose the married couple of kennel number two. They were in Delaware. The website said they had a dog for adoption. I emailed.

In her reply the owner mentioned how timid the animal was, that she would hide if company came over, and she needed to be a one-person dog. I was one person; I knew that much. Her age was two-and-a-half. (See my unprayed prayer list.) Since the couple couldn't show her because of her timid personality, they were looking to find a home for her. (See number three.) She ended her response, "There is no adoption fee for this dog."

I went to Delaware.

She was so beautiful I could hardly believe it. Despite her reputation she came right to the door, let me pick her up onto my lap and kissed me. They had given her what I thought was a terrible name (I won't tell you). "Oh, don't change it," the owners advised. The minute we got in the car I began calling her Chloe.

Our first couple of weeks were a nightmare. Chloe was not housebroken and had never been on a leash. I lost seven pounds walking her, trying to get her to go potty outside. They had told me she was crate trained, and I mistook Murphy's old cage for a crate. Until I discovered the difference, I had an adorable dog scared to death and covered with poo every time I came home. I didn't exactly love her yet, and I was getting ready to give up.

Driving to an afternoon nursing home visit, I called a friend whom I knew would tell me "It's okay" to take Chloe back. She didn't answer. I arrived at the activities office at work on the verge of tears. The staff women listened quietly as I poured out my tale of woe. Then they united their hearts in sisterhood and burst out laughing.

"My son tried to bite me when I left him at nursery school this morning!" Each of them had young children. I had no maternal experience whatsoever, and their laughter was telling me that this was what all mothers go through—even, it would seem, dog mothers.

Since it was so risky to leave her at home, I decided to take Chloe with me to my Sunday afternoon nursing home where I led a Bible hymn sing. I sat her on a chair next to me and blocked her escape with the neck of my guitar. But Chloe never moved. She sat still and quiet as could be for the entire hour. That's when I realized God had a plan for this dog. (I'm sure you don't want me to reference the prayer list again.)

I wondered what I could invent to take Chloe with me to the homes. Some kind of rolling cart? Something with wheels that I could fold up and take in the car? While I was trying to be creative someone told me about dog strollers. Oh. Who knew?

Once she learned, the hard way, that she was attached to the stroller with a leash, Chloe's own little ministry adventure began. She went from afraid-of-everything to spoiled-almost-rotten in a very short period of time. *"Gee, every time I meet someone, I get a treat. I guess people are not so bad."* Then there was the discovery of her incredible mind: "Say 'God bless you' in Russian!" *Woof!*

Brilliant. "Say 'I love you' but say it in French!" *Woof!* Amazing. I could go on and on.

Chloe can "open doors no man can shut" (Revelation 3:8) when we go room to room for our music visits. Sometimes I will see the beginning of a "no" forming on someone's lips that will change to an "ohhh" upon seeing that face in the stroller. People who are deaf whom I could never reach with song will light up and put out their hands for her. Even though it's obvious that she can't, Chloe has been given credit for singing *and* playing the guitar from seemingly sane individuals. I just drive the car. Her feet can't reach the pedals.

A staff woman shared about a resident we visited only once a month. He had recently passed away, and the week he was dying, he stretched out his hands and said, "Where's Chloe? I want my Chloe...."

If you find that hard to believe, I understand. But remember our prayers. God picked the perfect dog, and she came with His plan. The gift of Chloe was never meant for only me. She touches countless hearts and God uses her. Maybe not like He uses you and me, but He's the God of all the living. Is there anything too wonderful for Him?

When you did awesome things that we did not expect...Since ancient times no one has heard, no ear has perceived, no eye has seen any God besides you, who acts on behalf of those who wait for him.
Isaiah 64:3a, 4

4

Jesus on the Main Line

"Jesus on the main line, tell Him what you want!"
(Traditional)

Every Christmas season Chloe and I make our annual visit to my dear friend Miriam's family farm.

Miriam is a semi-retired missionary who devotes much of her time to caring for her elderly mother. For years, Miriam and other family members have taken turns rallying around this precious saint so that she might finish her days on the rolling farm she loves.

On this particular visit, Miriam, her mother, Chloe, and I spent a sweet hour laughing and singing together, my portable speaker blaring so her mom could hear to sing along. She remembered almost every word to the deep, old hymns.

The weather was icy enough that I'd slid all the way down their roller-coaster driveway and up to the house on arrival, skidding into place with some fear at the top. It never occurred to me that the return trip might be even harder.

When it was time to leave, we said our goodbyes, had our respective potties, and were all settled in the car with snacks for the long journey home. But once we left our perch above the driveway's plunge, access to the main road proved unattainable.

My first attempt to reach the road fell miserably short. So, I slid backwards down and up to the house again to gain momentum for another try. Praying no one would be coming, I "gunned it," thinking I could make it with a stick shift. But ice is no respecter of gears. I began another backwards slide, but this time I was spinning. A tree swung around in my rearview mirror. (I hadn't remembered a tree in the middle of the driveway.) Mercifully, I landed just beside it, solidly stuck in the very wet snow and mud.

I walked Chloe back up to the house to look for Miriam, who thought we were already well on our way. After praying together, she phoned every big, strong man she could think of. Only one answered; we wondered how much help one man could be in this situation.

Then I called the Auto Club. The driver arrived in a fast fifty-two minutes. I am sharing a bit of sarcasm with you.

"Sorry, hon, I can't help you, I can't go off the road." *(If I were on the road I wouldn't need you.)* I don't have chains long enough, hon, I'm really sorry. You need to call Royce Towing, hon, they can tow you out." *(Please stop calling me "hon" if you can't help me, dear.)*

Google reached Royce. I left a measured and minutely detailed message as befitting my maturity in Christ. "Help, please help, help, I'm stuck!" At five o'clock on a Sunday, they were closed.

Ten minutes later, up high on the glorious road of hope there appeared a gleaming flat-bed tow truck with "Royce" written in cursive on the side.

Once again displaying the self-control that is the fruit of the Spirit, I was jumping and clapping my hands. "Oh, hooray, you got here so fast, you got my message!"

"I didn't get any message. I just pulled someone else out and saw you down there as I was going by, so I thought I'd stop."

Pause for effect.

"Oh, you got a message alright, it just wasn't from me. The Lord Jesus called you!" At the end of my rope, I was swinging up and yelling down from a dizzying height for all to hear.

And there was an "all." It had turned into a towing party. Two sweet policemen ("You're not going to ticket me, are you?") parked on either side of the driveway's exit, their cars' flaming swords flashing a warning to those passing up on the slippery street. Miriam's nephew, the one man who had answered our call, stood overlooking. I was pumping everyone's hand and thanking them for coming to the event, and even had a nice chat with the youngest policeman about detective shows, citing some of my favorites while we watched the blessed chains of life reach down the hillside to my car. Of course I told him that the Lord had called the truck.

"I sing in nursing homes," I babbled, "this is Chloe, she goes with me in a stroller, do you know this song? I learned it from the folks in my Cleveland home." Then I serenaded him, "Jesus on the main line, tell Him what you want! Call Him up and tell Him what you want!"

Honestly, I've often looked down on that song from the narrow bridge of my nose, claiming a better theology. We know the Lord is not a vending machine.

But sometimes it's downright prudent to take a page out of someone else's songbook.

When I had first landed at Miriam's, *Fill Up Now* was flashing on the dashboard, with forty miles remaining. Mind you, I had run the engine for over an hour to keep Chloe warm before our hero Mr. Royce came to our rescue. But when I turned the key to leave, I watched the gas gauge rise to a full notch above empty. The computer had changed its mind, generously deciding to give us seventy-five more miles.

Did the slant of the hill fool the gauge into thinking my fuel level had doubled? I'll let you decide. *Neither do I exercise myself with great matters or in things too high for me* (Psalms 131:1).

And however you might explain how we got there, my car had undeniably been deposited up on the blessed highway at 6:00 pm that Sunday night. Chloe was seat-belted and sweetly tucked in under a Christmas blanket, the snacks were still on the floor, and we were happily headed home.

Our Father knows the difference between a cry of faith and a demand of presumption. Of course we know the Lord is not a vending machine. *Who hath directed the Spirit of the LORD, or being his counsellor hath taught him?* (Isaiah 40:13). But I also know this, and I will say it with the certainty of scripture: For His children, God is always right beside the phone.

And call upon me in the day of trouble:
I will deliver thee, and thou shalt glorify me.
Psalms 50:15

5
Perfect

She was the sun, I was the moon.

I existed to be a reflection of my mother; I have told you that she used her children. My role was to meet all of her emotional needs and to make sure that everyone saw her shine. Any time I did a bad job of reflecting, I felt the heat of her wrath. She took her love away and it felt like dying.

This was no task for an amateur. Her standards were impossibly high. Nothing less than a perfect performance was acceptable.

You know how sometimes if children need glasses, they don't realize it? They just think everyone sees the way they do. They've nothing to compare with, so how would they know? That's how it was with my childhood. How would I have known that things weren't the way they were supposed to be, that my life wasn't normal? But children blame themselves, children internalize conflict. I was in therapy a long time before I understood my mother to be mentally ill. All my life I thought there was something wrong with me.

But I must have thought I could learn the perfect child performance, and since there were no options, I tried and tried. Until, in my teens, I turned and tried something for myself. Then! Down came my world like a house of cards.

I remember lying in bed night after night, being so afraid of God because He surely knew the truth about me. He knew I wasn't good enough. I was afraid to go to sleep because of my overwhelming fear of dying. My teen years were a sloppy, fearful, sin-and hate-filled mess with alcohol and men already on their way. But men and alcohol didn't help. Neither did singing in bars.

Surprisingly enough, when I was about sixteen some well-meaning person—whose name I cannot remember—took me to a church. The subject of the sermon that morning was someone's misguided grandmother.

The pastor explained that despite her sweetness and faithful church attendance, that precious nana would not be going to heaven. At his conclusion, he gave us all the opportunity that the grandmother seemed to have missed. But first we had to identify ourselves.

"Raise your *hand* if you have guilt or *shame!* Raise your *hand* if you want to be *saved* and go to heaven!"

He was looking right at me. Apparently he had some secret theological insight.

With my heart pounding and my cover blown, my hand went up of its own accord. In front of everyone, he called me to come forward to the altar to kneel and pray a prayer. If I was worried about what to say, I needn't have been.

"Say these words," he commanded, and so I did. A little crowd gathered around me as the pastor proclaimed that I was going to heaven and had been born again.

I wanted to believe that I had just escaped the fires of hell, but none of it made sense to me. I had no understanding of Christ and his work, no repentance, and also no faith. But the pastor assured me that it was all true and solemnly handed me a silver dollar as if to crown his conviction. I assumed it was some kind of an award.

For about two weeks, I attempted to be a Christian—until I could no longer fool myself. I knew I hadn't been born again. Nothing had happened to me. It was easy enough to quit my new monastic lifestyle, and if I'd had any previous doubts about the sanity of these church people, I was then firmly convinced that they were all out of their minds. Especially the proponents of being "born again."

I quickly returned to my go-to escape habits of music, alcohol, and men, all of which stayed with me and took on strength in adulthood, bringing with them new permissions. That's just what adults do, right?

In my thirties, I again fell in with Christians during my stint as activities director. First came Ron, the former minister, who was hired to be my assistant. Then, after my unplanned departure (I was fired) I joined Ron's Bible study to stay in touch with him. Although initially suspicious of the entire little group, I soon began to like them and made exceptions for them when they spoke of being saved and born again. They were sweet. They didn't know any better.

Since I was more enlightened than they were, I eventually left them and my entire life to move to New Jersey and into my unemployed boyfriend's house. I did this, of course, in order to rescue him. Just another in a long line of messes I made all by myself, over and over again. But no sooner in, than I had to get out. There was so much abuse, it may have been worse than the house I grew up in.

I made one friend in New Jersey. Actually, she made the friendship and dragged me into it. She worked in the first nursing home that hired me in the Garden State, and the first words out of her mouth after hello were, "Are you *saved*?"

I was so tired of arguing about that awful word that seemed to follow me everywhere. In defeat I hung my head and muttered "I don't know," as my last, pathetic defense. She comforted me by patting my shoulders and assuring me that *she* thought I was saved. Apparently she had some secret theological insight.

She invited me to her church because they were "putting on a show." Not in the barn like in some old 1940s black-and-white, this platform was a megachurch of three thousand members. They had everything, including a dry ice machine.

I was insufferably critical of course, coming as I was from the show business perspective. But they did all right, for a church. For the grand finale the pastor came out wearing an expensive suit and a goatee. He looked like Satan. I distrusted him with my entire being.

The pastor talked about salvation and heaven and told everyone to bow their heads and pray. Oh yes, I remembered the prayer from when I was sixteen. Once again, I obeyed and asked Jesus into my heart.

"While all eyes are closed, raise your hand if you prayed," he instructed. I figured I'd better be honest.

My theological friend must have peeked. She saw my hand and pulled me up front, pushing me toward the pastor.

"Pastor, Susan just got SAVED!" Oh, boy.

"Wait! Now, just a minute, I don't know about that…" my mouth was off and running and the chip on my shoulder was bouncing like mad. Nobody was going to get me "saved," not if I could help it. I knew it was a lie.

We had a "discussion" in which I doubted everything and understood nothing he said. He gave me a cassette tape of his teaching (that's how long ago this was). I threw it out the car window on my way home.

Once my temper died down, a different kind of doubt crept in. This was the second time I had supposedly been saved. I wondered if something had finally happened to me.

Two weeks later, bent on rescuing myself from my abusive boyfriend's house and needing to secretly buy a paper (that's how long ago this was) to look for an ad for an apartment, I agreed to go back with my only friend to her megachurch for a regular service. The third one, the eleven o'clock. The most sensible time, at least.

At the finale of that service—here we go again—the pastor spoke of an argument he'd had two weeks earlier with a woman he called "Madame X." He quoted her word for word. Now he had my complete attention. He was talking about me.

Reaching around my jaw which had dropped to my knees, I nudged my friend. "He's talking about me!" was my stage whisper.

He boldly repeated my words to his congregation, and then he boldly rebuked them. He explained to all one thousand people, for the third time that morning, what Madame X had been doing wrong. And Madame X was now hanging on his words.

"Madame X had been trying to pray her way to heaven!"

(That's what he'd told me to do.)

"Madame X had been trusting in her own righteousness!"

(I had no idea what "righteousness" meant.)

Now came the real finale.

"When we stand before a holy God and we are covered by the blood of Jesus, God doesn't see our sin. He sees His perfect son."

Perfect. I was stunned by the word. Like a healing wind, it swept all the way back through my childhood, and in one remarkable moment encompassed the entirety of my life. The earth didn't stop, the ground didn't shake, but something lifted off of my shoulders and left me wondering why no one had ever told me this before.

Growing up, church fit my mother's image requirements; it made us look good. So my family had sporadically attended a "respectable" church (I would need another rating to explain those scare quotes to you). There, during every sermon, I was repeatedly reminded that Jesus died for my sins. As I got older, that idea only compounded my guilt. As I saw it, I was accountable for the death of Christ; it was just something else I'd done wrong.

I had never heard—nor understood—what faith in His sacrifice accomplished. It's as if as a child I believed it was me hanging on that cross. I was the one responsible for saving everyone in my family—and I was the one who had failed.

But sitting beside my friend in the megachurch that morning, God used the pastor's words to pull the nails, and He released me from that cross. To my wonderment, I realized that the perfect one had never been me. Just as I'd always feared, God knew that little girl wasn't good enough. But who could have imagined—Jesus is good enough in my place. He makes me perfect in the sight of God.

That, to the best of my knowledge, was the morning of my salvation. Yessir, born again. What beautiful words. And what a beautiful Savior who would do the impossible for me.

I went forward one more time. I just had to say something to the nice pastor. He greeted me, "Oh my goodness, I saw you out there this morning!"

Well, praise God you didn't change your message, Pastor. Susan just got saved.

For by one offering he hath perfected forever them that are sanctified.
Hebrews 10:14

"In New Jersey" (my first Christian song)
God lives in New Jersey,
That must be why I'm here.
I thought I was following you, but
That's just what He knew I would do.
He plans all the highways,
Circles are what He likes.
You just have to learn how to yield, and
Practice being one with the wheel, when you
Turn, turn turn.
I left Pennsylvania,
Yes I had a friend there,
But I never did have a home, so
I came to the Garden State alone.
Oh...
In my bed at night I face the highway when I sleep.
Traffic makes the rise and fall, the white noise of the deep.
Big rigs roll like thunder out to sea...
One-one-thousand, two-one-thousand, how far away?
Three-one-thousand, four-one-thousand,
How far away from me now?
In New Jersey...
Love can make you foolish,
Even feel embarrassed,
If you give up all you possess
On a bad bet, even this God can bless,
And he'll take you where you never would guess—
God lives in New Jersey.
–Susan Piper, "In New Jersey," *God Songs*

6
Too Much God

My time as activities director had brought much of me to my senses, and I was finally writing songs again. Amazingly, and at long last, a local folk label offered me my very first recording contract. I was certain I had arrived.

But Christ is the Master Interrupter, isn't He? No sooner had I finished recording my second CD with that label than He converted me to Himself.

Allow me to share a mental image that seems to define the Story of My Life:

> *Picture the rickety cart of Time Itself careening downhill at breakneck speed, piled high to overflowing with the moments and milestones of my experience. Now watch me chasing after it, running always a day or a year behind, frantically waving my arms and yelling, "Wait! Come back! I get it now!"*

After painfully extricating myself from the grip of my latest abusive boyfriend, I rented a little house on a divided highway in New Jersey, the State of my salvation. My soul may have met her savior, but the rest of me was dragging her heels. I was still drinking, involved with men, and dressing in a manner unbecoming a child of God. But I read the Word daily, attended the megachurch, and started writing songs about Christ. Not surprisingly, God used His gift of songwriting for my sanctification.

I wrote like crazy, new songs all about Him. Someone once told me I had been writing by myself too long. That was no compliment, but there was a reason I had always written alone. It was much too personal of a process for me to include anyone else. Now it seemed I had a partner. The Lord was deeply invading my privacy, even the place where the songs come from. I had never been so connected to anyone. In His great kindness, God reached to me in music.

> *I turned my head in shame,*
> *I said "No, You mustn't touch me.*
> *You don't know where I've been,*
> *If You knew, You wouldn't want me."*
> *He was so tender to me,*
> *Ever gently bending.*
> *Love came down to me,*
> *Love came down,*
> *I had no hope to reach to Him,*
> *So love came down.*
> –Susan Piper, "Love Came Down," *God Songs*

I visited my producer to tell him the news.

While he paced around his studio, I shared the details of my newfound faith. Clearly, he was not impressed. But with all the untried determination of a new believer, I persevered. Picking up my guitar, I made it halfway through my newest song before he put up his hand to stop me.

"I cannot support you in this," he said flatly. *And lo, thou art unto them as a very lovely song of one that hath a pleasant voice, and* can play well on an instrument: for they hear thy words, but they do them not* (Ezekiel 32:33). I cried all the way home.

I called the men who owned the record label and set up a meeting at a local restaurant. Clutching my demo of *God Songs* under the table, I nervously explained that "something had happened to me" in a church.

"You mean, like born again?" The bigger man leaned forward. I nodded with a small amount of embarrassment, wondering if my producer had turned informant and called ahead.

"Oh, we wouldn't be allowed back in our homes if we recorded something like that!" These were two Jewish men. "You never signed the contract for the second CD; let's just let it go at that." And I was fired.

It was humbling to realize how dispensable I was. The problem of any contract complications was quickly resolved, and I was once again out in the cold as far as recording went. During a prayerful walk in the woods, I was reminded of Christ being led out to the wilderness after His baptism. *Please don't abandon me here*, I prayed.

> *It's You who made the tree,*
> *The tree that holds the limb I'm standing on.*
> *You can calm the wind,*
> *The wind that threatens everything I own.*
> *I'm holding on too tight,*
> *You want me to keep my fingers open.*
> *And this is the extent of the faith I have,*
> *I'm frightened and I'm so ashamed to say,*
> *There won't be any mountains changing places now,*
> *They're right here in my way.*
> *But you are able to keep me from falling...*
> –Susan Piper, "From Falling," *God Songs*

Performing was now uncharted territory. I was attempting to merge my old and new lives, and the transition was a bit bumpy. I knew I'd have to change my playlist and drop my in-between-songs banter filled with sarcasm and innuendo, but what could I sing and what should I say instead? Was I allowed to be funny? How funny?

I am not good at gray; it causes me too much tension. I've been black and white all my life. At a gig for the Library Association around this time (the little room was charming; it may even have been a former church), I received a bad or rave review, take your pick: "We don't want you to come back again. Everyone said it was too much God."

My new direction had been sealed.

I have never been successful at my music as the world defines success. I've yet to hear my songs on Christian radio or receive a royalty check. Although the Lord has provided for seven CDs of my songs about Him, many copies remain in my closet. Ambition dies hard; I'm not sure I have killed it and I'm not sure I must. But as I pray for continued usefulness, I remember how small Christ's earthly ministry often appeared to be. We do what we can with what we have been given; we trust the results to Him.

> *We go on,*
> *When we have to spend the money,*
> *When it takes too long,*
> *When the world says, "No."*
> *What we don't understand*
> *Will one day be revealed to us,*
> *We go on,*
> *'Cause the Lord says, "Go."*
> –Susan Piper, "We Go On," God Is

7
Love-Hate Relationship

We humans are such gloriously complicated beings.

Our Creator displays His incomparable genius in our bodies, capabilities, and emotions. We, in turn, look at ourselves in the mirror and decide we emerged from the slime millions of years ago and have magically evolved into present-day creatures who conceive life, give birth, go to the bathroom, cry, and love. We must have lost the sanity gene somewhere in the first million years.

Our brokenness is conspicuously displayed in daily life. Our common sense is missing, too. The longer we inhabit our planet, it seems, the lower the common denominator falls. One quick trip to Wal-Mart proves my point.

The Bible—the Word of God and the Christian's history book/family tree—minces no words about our fallen situation. Sin is reported straight-up: horrific deaths and espionage and blood and guts, they're all in there. (If little boys knew, they'd take an interest in the Bible much earlier in life.)

But of course, the glory is there, too, the big Glory, capital "G." See our Wonderful Savior on His white horse, conquering death by dying and conquering sin by becoming it, turning the world as we knew it upside down as He rises up from His grave, leaving a trail of Life in His wake.

A friend who is firmly grounded in the Lord once gave me an "assignment," as she called it. She sent me a commonly accepted truism that reads like the faulty thinking of the world, of unbelievers who hang out with Freud and his slimy mates. I couldn't imagine the reason for her sudden fascination with psychology, but maybe she was trying to help someone who was confused. And since she asked if I could prove the idea with Scripture, I was willing to try.

Here's her "truism": *You have to love yourself before you can love someone else.*

Yes, I have heard that. And I used to believe it. But before I dismissed it and labeled it hogwash, I thought maybe I'd better double-check. My friend isn't slimy, but she might be sneaky enough to want me to think about something for my own good. What if the someone she was trying to help was me?

So, I opened my Bible and started searching.

Step one: define "Love yourself." There's a long drop off that first step, if you ask me, which she did. So, I'm thinking...do I love myself? Doesn't everyone? Some people hate themselves. Some people seem to do both.

Now, where does love come from? Not from the million-year-old slime. Love comes from God (1 John 4:7). But there are ways to love oneself that are actually hatred in disguise. And vice versa.

The demon-possessed man in Mark 5:1-20 could be described as full of violent self-hatred, desiring only to harm himself and fend off the repeated attempts to help him. No one could bind him, no one could tame him, the Scripture says.

On the other hand, we might say he loved himself because he did what he desired. He could have left the tombs and run to the priest for exorcism. Instead, he dug into his isolation and fought off the intervention crews that tried to get him out.

But certainly, a stronger Man was needed, to bind his mighty self-will and the will of the Legion of demons inside him. No mere

Freudian intervention would cut the mustard here. So Jesus sent the spirits into the swine, and they rushed into the sea.

As the dead pigs bobbed in the water, the man was restored to his right mind. He was released from his sin, his very-real demons, and himself. Now who does he love?

He pleads to go with Jesus. He desperately wants to be where Jesus is. His first sane thoughts are to attach himself to the One who takes his mind off himself. He loves his Jesus, and in this, for the first time, he truly loves himself.

Then Jesus gives him his own assignment: *"Go home to thy friends, and tell them how great things the Lord hath done for thee, and hath had compassion on thee"* (Mark 5:19).

And he departed, and began to publish in Decapolis how great things Jesus had done for him: and all men did marvel (Mark 5:20). Now he begins to love others; he tells them about his Jesus.

It is the new order of love—the upside-down of health and Life that Christ brings the world—that makes all the difference here. *We love Him, because He first loved us* (1 John 4:19). I don't need to love myself before I can love you. I don't even know what love is.

The love of God is shed abroad in our slimy hearts, and they are lifted up to Glory, capital "G." In His light we see light, and the darkness of the tombs is dispelled. I once was self-destructive and blind, but now I see the love of my Creator. And His love for me makes me love Him, run after Him, all other loves paling. If I cannot be with Him now, I will content myself with telling you again and again how beautiful He is, how much He has done and continues to do for me. And this is the way I will love you, and this is the way I will love myself—very, very well.

...that ye, being rooted and grounded in love,
May be able to comprehend with all saints
what is the breadth, and length, and depth, and height;
And to know the love of Christ, which passeth knowledge,
that ye might be filled with all the fullness of God.
Ephesians 3:17b-19

8
Changes

I sang and played guitar at my brother's wedding and got drunk at his reception. I was fifteen.

My parents drank and had a well-stocked liquor cabinet. While they were out one day I got into it and was passed out on the sofa when they came home. "The house could have burned down," my mother said.

Where I came from, you just had to ask, and someone would buy you a bottle. Getting it open could be tough, however. I remember being at the local park with a pen knife trying to chip the cork out of something cheap. Very tedious. And not even very good.

Since I was still underage at that point, my parents had to go into the city with me for my gigs in the bars. I had the perfect formula for success: I was only fifteen (going on thirty-five) and wrote songs that could break your heart in three-and-a-half minutes flat. The bartenders hovered over me like raptors, always ready to add something extra to my ginger ale. I don't know the statute of limitations for the crime of serving alcohol to a minor. But if I could get my hands on one of those men today, I would do my best to put his claws behind bars.

After I left home I drank daily, but usually at night and by myself—with a few loud and embarrassing exceptions. I made a good appearance; I don't think many suspected my habit. I alternated between liquor stores to avoid getting on a first-name basis with the clerks.

Unless disaster struck or if I was traveling and needed something strong in a small bottle to tuck into my suitcase, I usually drank wine. It's perfectly acceptable, as long as no one knows how many empty bottles are clinking around in your trash.

I would always drink until I felt a buzz. It really didn't matter whether my mood was high or low; I drank to dull the intensity of my emotions. If I'd had a good show, I would tell myself that I was celebrating. In reality, I had to wind down from all that love that disappeared the minute I left the stage.

I quit once for two whole weeks to prove to myself that I could do it. Point proved, I was free to return to my normal ways.

When I first came to Christ, I had no idea my life was supposed to change. I don't remember seeing a verse that said "thou shalt not live a promiscuous life and thou shalt not drink until you are buzzed every night." Yes, that message is all through the Bible, but nothing had jumped out at me. I was brand new.

As far as the men went, one day I just had the great revelation that God doesn't like sex outside of marriage. I didn't know how I'd arrived at the conclusion, but I believed it was true.

But the wine? I did develop a nagging worry that not everyone was leaving Bible study to drink when they got home. But it was my most reliable friend. I didn't want to let it go. I'd heard smoking was a greater addiction, so I prayed the way I imagined a smoker would: "Lord, please take away the desire." It was a bit cowardly, but it was a start.

However, my location was against me. I was converted in New Jersey, and the selling point of the state (to me) was that you could buy wine any day of the week, even Sunday. The closest store was less than two miles away.

One afternoon, the parking lot was crawling with some new and unpleasant guests. A dirty and dangerous-looking little mob had set up camp by the entrance door. I didn't know what they were up to, but I could feel their eyes on me as I hurried past. Once inside, I was stopped short by the smell. As a frequent customer, I knew the store had never smelled bad before. Looking around, I saw that everything looked dirty—the floor, the shelves, even the empty cardboard boxes. I remembered my prayer.

I had very carefully asked God to take away my desire, but not my drink. His response was every bit as specific. God didn't touch the wine. Instead, He ruined my experience of buying it—from the parking lot to the liquor store itself.

You would think that would have been enough to stop me. But in my bondage, the best that I could offer Him was a bargain: "Lord, I'll go without it one night." I picked a Bible study night, which would bring me home about nine. I would have two hours of sobriety until bedtime. I drank milk. I didn't sleep well.

In the morning, I woke with this in my mind: *First Timothy three three*. Being new to the Bible, I didn't know about the two Timothies yet. I also didn't know that the Holy Spirit would bring Scripture to my mind. But in this case, He gave me nothing more than the reference, forcing me to look it up myself. Which I finally did. It was the element of surprise that set fire to God's words. When I read them, they hit my heart like a perfectly aimed bolt of lightning: *not given to drunkenness...* (1 Timothy 3:3 NIV).

The word "drunkenness" here means "wine."

He knew. Well, of course He knew, but He really knew, and He obviously didn't like it. They say the best thing to help an addict is a healthy fear of God. Suddenly I had that.

But do remember how long I'd lied to myself, and in case you don't know this (yet), let me tell you I am extremely stubborn. I dropped the wine immediately. Then I considered casually picking it back up. You know, just socially. I can drink socially, can't I?

Addicts can't.

A friend came to dinner, and of course he brought wine. We only drank half the bottle, and the other half was back in the refrigerator waiting for the next social occasion. In the morning, I was on my spot on the sofa with my Bible. There was a lot of unrest coming from the kitchen.

Now, I am not telling you that I hallucinated or even had a vision. It was more like a strong cartoon impression in my mind. I could picture that refrigerator rocking back and forth, I could "hear" things rattling and rolling, and I knew if I didn't do something, it would explode. I ran in, threw open the door, pulled out the bottle, uncorked it, and dumped it down the drain. And that was truly the end of that. June 2001, right before my baptism and nine months after my new birth. I was finally free.

Living in Ohio now, I find liquor everywhere. It's not that I am never tempted, but by His grace I live like a Nazarite (I do cut my hair). I have a mantra of gratitude that helps me:

> In the grocery store going through the massive wine display to get to the bread:
> *Thank you, Lord Jesus.*
> Passing the cases of beer to find the eggs:
> *Thank you, Lord Jesus.*
> Stopping at the mini-mart for milk on the way home, where is the milk? All the way in the back corner surrounded by all the other bottles:
> *Thank you, Lord Jesus.*

In a state where you can buy guns, liquor, and bait on every corner, it's a wonder the people and fish have survived. But thus far hath the LORD helped us.

Thank you, thank you, LORD Jesus.

Draw me, we will run after thee:
the king hath brought me into his chambers:
we will be glad and rejoice in thee,
we will remember thy love more than wine:
the upright love thee.
Song of Solomon 1:4

9
You Can Do It

"It'll never make the hit parade."

I doubt that my father ever even remembered his critique of my blossoming teen-aged songwriting. But if I live to be a hundred and forget my own name, I will remember his words until the day I die. It takes a lot of stubbornness to overcome a stamp of disapproval like that. Thankfully, as my therapist often noted, I am the most stubborn person on the face of the planet.

But I had an encourager once. I had her for the last eight years of her life and the first of mine in Christ.

Aunt Pearl was eighty-nine when we met, the relative of an ex-boyfriend. I dropped him and took her. You know a lot about me by now; you can guess she was the much better choice.

She might have been four feet tall. Osteoporosis had bent Pearl's already tiny frame and given a hunch to her shoulders. It hadn't hunched her personality, though. She was a little ball of fire with a very strong will and mind. I used to tell her if I'd known her in her youth I could never have kept up.

When her husband of sixty-eight years died, I began phoning her at the same time every evening. She was always home; the predictability of my call was just for her reassurance. I had learned that from my co-worker Ron. After I was fired from my activities director position, he'd called me every day at noon, and you can bet I was waiting by the phone. Just five minutes made a big difference to me as I battled the isolation of unemployment and the struggles of carving out a new life's work for myself. So it was with Aunt Pearl; our regular calls brought us into a real friendship.

In the beginning I called at nine p.m. Then, as she aged (more), we moved it up to seven. If I missed a day or was doing something that kept me from the phone, I'd come home to a lilting message on my machine. "Suuusaaan, Aunt Pearl. Did ya forget about me? I thought you might have fallen in a hole somewhere. Caaaall me...." Then she would pause, her voice would soften, and the melody would take on another little lift. "I loooove ya." I have several precious voices on my answering machine that are recorded for eternity. Why didn't I save hers?

During every evening's call I would read the Bible to her. If I forgot, she would remind me. I was concerned about her because Pearl's religion taught that good works are necessary for salvation. Not that they necessarily follow after, as the Bible teaches everywhere, but that they are necessary to obtain it, which the Bible teaches nowhere. Upon hearing that Jesus called his disciples to leave their fishing nets and follow him, Pearl demanded, "What happened to all the fish?" She'd lived through the depression; she was very practical.

On Sunday afternoons I would pick Pearl up in Northeast Philly and take her for a ride through a park I had stumbled upon, one blessed spot of green in all that concrete. I'd roll down her window, hit my flashers, and drive on the shoulder at five miles an hour—angering everyone behind me—so she could admire all the "stand-alone houses" and comment on the rich people who must live in them. She was so tiny she didn't even set off the airbag sensors in my car. I'd tease her and say a Thanksgiving turkey weighed more than she did. She didn't mind. She loved me.

Aunt Pearl was my introduction to the Great Northeast. Hers was the first Philly rowhome I'd ever been in. I found her neighborhood very depressing, along with the dark interior of her row. Of course, that's where I later bought my first house, a row, in a neighboring section. Home ownership was very important to Pearl. She would give me money gifts for my birthday and Christmas, following my thank yous with "I know you rent, Susan."

As a new Christian I had a lot to say about Christ and didn't worry much about discernment. I would just start spouting, and Aunt Pearl imagined me a preacher. "There she goes again. Get out your soapbox, Susan, I can see you standing on a street corner somewhere!" But no matter what I attempted, Aunt Pearl would always tell me, "You can do it, Susan, I know you can." If you could bottle that and sell it, you never would.

When the record company fired me for my conversion to Christ, Aunt Pearl happily took on the position of Temporary Record Executive. Without discrimination, she welcomed listening to my new songs as fast as I could write them, as well as the old hymns which were all new to me.

Obviously, Aunt Pearl was not familiar with the expense (she would have been horrified) of self-recording my music. I tried to explain the requirements of my new situation to her, introducing the concept of "fundraising concerts." The afternoon before the first of such events, she asked me to stop by to see her.

As I climbed her concrete steps, Pearl's front door swung open like that of an ancient crypt, mysteriously summoning me inside. From the darkness a shadowy little figure emerged, one hand hidden behind her back. Silently extending her arm, she unfolded her fingers. A silver ring with tiny blue stones surrounding a small, antique-cut diamond lay in the palm of her hand.

Looking up at me, Aunt Pearl delivered a short recitation as if she'd practiced all morning in front of her mirror: "My parents gave me this for my sixteenth birthday. I would like very much for you to have it. I want to wish you every good success with your party." She did everything but curtsy.

Fundraising aside, it was no light thing for me to lose my record contract. Besides the financial support, gone were the connections, the opportunities, and the presumptions of talent that accompany a professional association. Starting from scratch, I began recording countless demos for Nashville executives. Even more funds were exhausted on twelve-hour road trips to the music city to hunt down publishers and agents. Computer-sitting became my newest hobby as I waited for "anyone" to get back to me. (Three follow-up emails later, "Are you *sure* Mr. So-and-So is still on vacation?") Oh, the humiliation.

If you look, wait, hope, and stare at your computer long enough for encouragement, you actually can fall into a hole somewhere. Suddenly all of your worth is hanging by strings attached to everyone else's fingers and you can't even lift one of your own because you just aren't good enough and you'd better stay in your hole forever. Oh, the disappointment.

Aunt Pearl knew about disappointment. She was disappointed in God.

I used to drive her to my church, the big church where the Lord had saved me. On the way one Sunday she confided in a low tone, "I've been very angry with God, Susan, because He didn't answer my prayer for Uncle Frank. He didn't let me keep him." When you love someone, sixty-eight years is not long enough.

The sermon title that morning was, "When God Says 'No'." This wasn't lost on Pearl; she shot me a knowing look. At the conclusion, prayers of healing were offered to anyone who wanted to come forward. The pastor announced that everyone would first be asked if they had received the Lord. I wanted to pick Pearl up and deliver her to the altar, but I outwardly held my peace and prayed. She said, "Let's go."

The Pastor's gentle wife bent over Aunt Pearl, asking softly, "Do you want to pray to receive Jesus?"

My knee was touching Pearl's. I will never forget: "Oh, yes I do."

As the years went by and her mind weakened, Aunt Pearl seemed to revert to her former religious ways, and my fears over her mistaken beliefs returned. Soon she became too frail for any discussion of Truth, and eventually, for any discussion at all. I tried hard to prepare myself, as if preparing could somehow protect me from my impending sorrow.

> *When I leave her small room the sky is still blue,*
> *Daylight is fading, the leaves are turning,*
> *This is my favorite time of year...*
> *But I know winter is coming.*
> *And it won't be long 'til the shadows find us,*
> *They turn back the hour as if to tell us,*
> *"Hold on to all the light you have...*
> *You know winter is coming."*
> *Soon there will be bitterness to steel my heart against,*
> *Icy winds to pound my chest and sting my eyes,*
> *And take my breath away...*
> –Susan Piper "Winter is Coming," *Living Things*

Days after she slipped into silence, God graciously gave Pearl a peaceful death at home. Hospice nurses were with her at the time, and I was home in bed with my Bible, waiting for the call.

I read, *For this God is our God for ever and ever: he will be our guide even unto death* (Psalms 48:14). I read it, but I'm not sure I believed it that night. I don't know why I was afraid to accept those words as assurance from the Lord for my dear Aunt Pearl.

Looking back, I think I was too hard on her and expected too much from her failing mental capacities. Old habits die so hard. Aunt Pearl may not have pulled free from every religious trapping, but with her mouth she confessed, and I think in her heart, she believed. I feel much more hopeful now that I will see her dear little self again.

If I let myself, I still miss her so. Pearl was my cheerleader. Unlike my critical father, her confidence rested on nothing more than my shoulders. Never mind what I would or would never accomplish. Aunt Pearl believed in me.

*But encourage one another daily,
as long as it is called "Today."*
Hebrews 3:13 NIV

10

Motherhood

"Our dad put a for-sale sign in our yard and we have to decide if we want to stay here with our stepmom, go live with our real mom in the Poconos, or go to Florida with our dad and his new girlfriend..."

Sitting on my sofa were twelve-year-old twins I had fallen in love with.

I never wanted children. I was afraid of them; I used to think that I didn't like them at all. Certainly, I had no basis for thinking of them positively. I didn't like myself as a child and didn't enjoy being one, although there's a case to be made that much of me still remains so. (I once told a friend that I wanted to decorate my home in a slightly more sophisticated, grown-up style. She said, "Well, you can try.")

Soon after my conversion I rented an upper apartment in the home of a very kind older couple who often brought dinner to my door. After work, I'd hear my doorbell ring and, with the flourish of a fancy headwaiter, the husband would present a portion of their supper from behind his back. "Dinner is served!"

Directly next door, and very close to us, was another kind of home that was noisily in the process of imploding. The couple had a new baby and twins, Max and Kacie, from the husband's previous marriage.

I don't remember how my friendship with the twins started. I imagine they were desperate for adult (even such as mine) companionship and approval, but I marveled that these children were so engaging. I could never predict what they would say. I didn't know they could be so much fun.

They loved my doorbell and suddenly, so did I. Up they came with a fifty-cent box of instant corn muffin mix. "Can we make this?" And there was Max, who had trouble pronouncing his "Rs," resting one freckled arm on their backyard gate, inviting a neighbor boy with a confident little swagger in his voice: "Wan' go chourch?"

Bravely, I took them with me on Sunday mornings, immediately aware of my driving habits. Now I was an example and had to wear my seat belt and slow down at the yellow lights. I was so proud of them, even though they weren't mine.

They took turns riding in the front seat, all of us buckled up. We would often hit McDonald's on the way home; I was a big spender and allowed them to order anything from the dollar menu, up to three dollars. I guess I didn't properly care for their nutrition, but they were neglected and thrilled to receive the attention, and I was in love and so happy to give it. They weren't used to church, of course; I was barely used to it myself. Coming home after a family-night dinner on a Wednesday evening I heard Max from the back seat, "How come everybody likes us?" I think I muttered something about the image of God and love in Christ—at least I hope I thought quickly enough for a question like that. But maybe I should have just told them how utterly likable they were.

Both of the twins were having trouble seeing in school and needed glasses, but no one seemed to be doing anything about it. I knocked on their front door and finally, officially, introduced myself to their father, of whom I was in fear. I offered to take them to the eye doctor. He said, "No." I heard him behind my back as I left, "I wish people would leave my children alone."

But now their parents were divorcing. There was a decision to be made, and somebody thought the children were the ones to make it. This would make the second divorce in their short lives. "My whole world is falling apart," Kacie said. I understood more than she knew.

I cried and prayed for them. They often heard me pray out loud. But they weren't my children, and there wasn't much else I could do.

Pulling up one day, I found them in their yard, next to that infamous sign, wearing their father's rubber boots and hauling trash bags as big as they were to the curb. It was time.

> *They're up to their middles*
> *In black plastic trash bags,*
> *Out in the backyard,*
> *Stuffing the mem'ries down*
> *Deep to the bottom,*
> *Where no one can find them,*
> *The things that once mattered*
> *Are history now...*

When I asked about their dog, Max put two hands together and leaned his head against them in the universal sign of "sleep." They left their cat behind in the metal tool shed. In the summer. My landlords adopted it in time.

However the decision was realized, they went to the Poconos to be with their mom. My church sent up a big wicker laundry basket full of Christmas gifts and I had the privilege of delivering it. I looked for a church up there and tried to connect them with one that had a youth group and maybe a basketball court. You know, something to help them find the Lord and keep them off the streets. I visited a couple of times, but they were too far away; I couldn't keep it up.

By now, I guess Max and Kacie could both be married with children of their own. It is frightening to think about. Because not only did I understand them and their perspective, sad to say, I understood their father's as well. His way of coping had once been mine. Things don't work out, relationships sour. You turn your back and try again, never mind if there are children. Go make a new family—just hope that the sins of the fathers don't follow you there.

God didn't give me children, but if I'd had any before His intervention in my life, I'm sure I would have done some serious damage to them. *But what I hate, that do I* (Romans 7:15). For that reason, I'm almost grateful I didn't have the opportunity.

But I do miss that feeling I'll never have, of being so connected to another life in this world. It's true I don't have the regret, but I'll never have the joy either. I'll never experience that kind of love. Don't you think that's sad? I do.

The consequences of my sin and that of others may have prevented me from entering the promised land of Motherhood. But from the lofty precipice of that little house apartment, I was given a glimpse of it from afar. I can be encouraged when I remember Max and Kacie. In their crisis God put them right next door to a brand-new Christian, and He is so purposeful in everything He does. They received something good from Him—something different—through the earthen vessels of me and my church. God had His wonderful hand upon them once, and it might rest upon them still—or again. The hope I carry for the twins is the certainty I keep for myself: In Him, the fatherless find mercy (Hosea 14:3).

...Living things,
Growing things,
Breathing things,
Wounded things...
Living things,
Precious things,
Are things you don't throw away.
–Susan Piper, "Living Things," *Living Things*

11

Martha and Me

Martha is a small brown bird
Who fell out of the nest,
To a geriatric cradle
To the local home of rest.
Little wings all twisted up
And pretzeled in the bed,
With a Pentecostal witness
Like a white dove on her head...

I was brand new in Christ when I met Martha. So brand new that I may have met her when I was still the same-old me.

The woman who dragged me to the church where I was saved worked at the facility that was Martha's home. It wasn't long before another Christian on staff heard about God's work in me and asked point blank about my conversion. (Apparently this nursing home was famous for hiring pushy Christians.) I was so very new; the chips had not quite fallen from my shoulders. "That's personal," I pushed back, cutting him off. None of his business. Today, I will witness to the point of embarrassment. That's how God changes a person.

Oh, Martha was a witness. Early on she told me the story of waking up one day, in her forties, unable to get out of bed. With fast and sinful living, she had been running from God, and He'd caught her. She'd called in the neighborhood children who clustered around her and told the little ones (and everyone else) the same thing:

> *"On my way to work one night,*
> *the Holy Spirit said to me,*
> *'Martha, stop everything that you're doing Baby,*
> *I want you for Myself!'"*

Rheumatoid arthritis had flattened her. Allergic to the treatments, she'd been in bed for thirty years.

> *Martha says, "It wasn't God*
> *Who did this thing to me.*
> *This is evident of evil,*
> *This is of the enemy."*
> *Jesus told him, "Take her bones,*
> *But save her soul for Me—*
> *I will handle her deliverance,*
> *And I will have My victory."*

Martha had had a career singing for the Lord with her siblings in a gospel group that traveled from church to church. By the time I met her, her voice had dropped below my own contralto. She sang her harmonies under me, which was very unusual for a woman.

We harmonized on her favorite hymn for Martha's entry in the nursing home beauty contest. This was a smashing event. The activities staff had collected formal attire from thrift stores and well-dressed donors. Fresh boutonnieres were pinned to the lapels of every man's suit or tuxedo. The women rediscovered their forgotten femininity, arrayed in the dresses of former bridesmaids and debutantes. Oh, the dignity that resurfaced in everyone's eyes. You just couldn't help but see "Mr. or Ms. Jones" in a brand-new light.

I have a framed picture taken of us on that day. Martha was in her Geri chair, all dressed up and draped in an evening gown with a big stuffed dog on her lap. She was focused on me, stooping beside her in my still-short skirt. We were a hit. She won the white banner that boasted "Most Spiritual" which then waved over her bed. Babe in Christ that I was, she certainly earned that apart from me.

How Martha managed to eat Tootsie Rolls with her dentures I can't say, but she was addicted and recruited me as her supplier. Instead of "Hello," she'd greet me with, "Did you bring the Tootsies, Baby?" And then would follow her standard post-visit dismissal, "Don't forget the Tootsies!"

Whenever I found Martha in a small group with other residents, I would show her off by singing the song I'd written for her. She was pleased, but she really preferred my lively children's songs. She memorized them all, requesting them by title, keeping time by raising her eyebrows up and down and wiggling her toes. She couldn't move much else. It was like singing for the Queen.

When she lost her daughter to lupus, Martha asked me to sing at the funeral. And what a funeral too, a real home-going celebration with stamping of feet and rejoicing. (I was new to Christ and His church back then, but even now, I can say I still haven't been in many churches like that. I will always be just a white woman from Ohio.) When it came time to sing, I couldn't see the congregation from where they'd positioned me on the altar. So, I voiced my complaint and shuffled my microphone stand sideways, while my guitar swung around my neck. Martha took great notice of that and quoted me when she saw me next. "I can't see Martha," she said with a smile.

Since I'd just been fired from my record company due to my conversion, I had to fundraise to record my first Christian CD. Martha prayed with me every step of the way. We imagined what it would be like if we could record a song together, as she and her biological sisters had done so long ago. The Lord had a little surprise in mind for Martha in answer to that prayer. When I met with Grant, my new producer, I asked if there was a way to include Martha on *God Is*. "Sure," he said, "I've done plenty of remote recording. We'll just go to the nursing home." Looking at his calendar, he picked the first convenient open date in January. On arriving we found Martha sitting up in her chair, ready to sing, draped in yet another formal gown. Of course she was dressed up. It was her birthday.

Grant set up in her room and recorded as we harmonized our award-winning hymn, "What a Friend We Have in Jesus." Then he asked Martha about her testimony, and off she went.

> "...and I do trust Him, and I always will, and I promised Him that I would never pass a soul without witnessing to them! If they'll stand still long enough, I got 'em! Oh, I gotcha! And when this tape goes out, everyone that ever hears it will be blessed and blessed. And they'll want to know more and more about you, Lord. In Jesus' name we pray. We love you, Lord. Amen."
> –from "Martha and Me," *God Is*, Susan Piper

But even the most loving connection with the dearest nursing home resident is tenuous. And when Martha died, I wasn't even told. I came to work after it was all over. "We looked for your CD for the funeral, but we couldn't find it," my boss said. The family had wanted to play Martha's testimony.

I'm sure Martha's family knew her words by heart, as did everyone who went to her home-going celebration. I know there was much rejoicing and stamping of feet, but I wasn't terribly sad that I'd missed it. I knew her in life, and that was my privilege. I will know her in Eternal Life as well. Her memorial card read, "Hallelujah! She suffers no more!"

Martha was a great encouragement to me as a new believer. She helped to fuel the fire the Holy Spirit was bringing to my soul. Following our visits (and the Tootsie Roll reminders), she would always pronounce her blessing, sailing it out the door and down the hall after me. I can still hear her words and picture them floating on a musical staff in the air: "Go to your destiny, Baby, go to your destiny!"

Touch and agree, touch and agree,
Go to your destiny,
Touch and agree, touch and agree,
Go to your destiny!
Borne for heaven,
Hear the sparrow pray as she sings
Borne for heaven,
Every prayer has wings.
–Susan Piper, "Wings," *God Songs*

12

My Father

...but the LORD had shut up her womb. And her adversary also provoked her sore, for to make her fret, because the LORD had shut up her womb.

I Samuel 1:6

There's no ambivalence here; Scripture is plainly certain. The LORD is the One who shut up Hannah's womb. Everyone believed it, including Hannah's adversary—her husband's other, more fruitful wife. That woman tormented Hannah.

The trouble with torment is that it can make us doubtful of God's motives. I can imagine the venomous spewings of Hannah's Greater Adversary, as he might have "helped" her along: *Why doesn't God give you a child? He could if He wanted to. Would a good God purposely shut your womb? He doesn't seem very loving to me....*

In Scripture, God often reveals His behind-the-scenes motives. We read that God remembered Hannah, that her special child was His gracious response to her persistent prayers. We are told that Samuel was the prophet-son, whose name means "heard of God," making his birth a kind of crowning for Hannah's faith, and all the more worth waiting for. The Bible spells out the backstory so clearly in black and white. In our daily lives, however, things can get muddy.

A while back, I was singing at a retreat where the guest speaker was a promoter of Open Theism. If you don't know, please don't even look it up. It's heretical and awful; bad doctrine. The short definition: Since it can be very challenging to believe a good God is in charge of even the bad things that happen, let's take away His glory and power so it's easy to believe He's good. Impotent, even ignorant, but good.

I was seated at the table with the retreat speaker and his wife. They shared that they had lost several babies. It was so terribly hard. That's when they adopted their new belief system (and took to writing books about it.) Because who could bear to think that God "ordaineth whatsoever cometh to pass" in their situation?

When it was time for me to sing and share, I used my opportunity to boldly proclaim the Sovereignty of God, quoting Scripture in my stories but subtly aiming my darts at the speaker's theology. When it was his turn to speak, he rebuked and corrected my "misunderstandings," aiming his own darts back at me. I don't know if the attendees knew what was going on, but I couldn't make eye contact with him by the end of the day. And I couldn't wait to get out of there. The saddest thing was, people were lining up to buy his books.

I may not have suffered the loss of a child, but we had a tragedy in our family, too—big enough to push my own theology into the mud. Our parents, long-since divorced, died two days apart at Christmastime. Our father's death was a suicide.

Now you may cringe at this, but from the onset, I had no trouble believing that God ordained even my father's death. I am very Reformed in my thinking, and I know that nothing can possibly happen unless God ordains it. My trouble with my father's suicide was that it brought me down on the other horn of the dilemma.

I knew God ordained it. But I didn't think that made Him very good.

This thinking, as you can imagine, had lowered a thick wet cloud over my spiritual life. Every time I heard Christians tell their happy Christian stories with their happy Christian endings, concluding with the proclamation that "God is *good*," I would nod my head with the rest. But in my spirit was a stumbling block of solid ice. I prayed and prayed, but it wouldn't go away. And I was afraid to tell anyone.

You see, ever since my breakdown and the turmoil of my teen years, I'd had little communication with my emotionally distant father. Even after I came to Christ, nothing improved. I saw him only once a year, and during each visit he would interview me endlessly about my mental health, repeating questions about my crisis as if he hadn't even been there when it happened. No matter how often I explained, it seemed he could never understand "what went wrong" back then. Bitter arguments escalating into battles would ensue. It was always the same.

One Thanksgiving, about five years before he died, we had just repeated our annual scenario. It was night, and I was about to relive my childhood by running away in the dark from Virginia and driving back to Pennsylvania. I made it as far as the front seat of my car before pulling out my phone. On the other end of the line, a dear friend counseled me to stay.

In the morning, when things had quieted down, my father drove me out to the docks to show me his boat. Sailing had become his obsession, and sadly, mattered more to him than anything in the world. As we stood on the deck, he asked me once again about my childhood: What happened? Again, I explained.

All of a sudden, the LORD opened his understanding, and he heard me for the first time in his life. He heard the lies my mother had told me, he believed the prison she had put me in, and he cried for the realization of it all. My father put his arms around me and pulled me to his chest, weeping as he asked, "Why didn't you come to me?" (As if as a child I could have; and as an adult I'd tried so many times.) In all sincerity he wondered why I'd withheld the truth for so long. But never mind, he heard me then. And my Heavenly Father poured love into my heart for him. God took away a wedge from between us that neither one of us had ever been able to move.

We never came to have the kind of relationship I'd hoped for. But from that time on, we were finally able to connect. It was night and day.

That's what was breaking my heart.

It was December, near the one-year anniversary of my father's death. While I was waiting for my car to be repaired, I had stopped around the corner to visit a lovely Christian family I didn't get to see very often. My girlfriend welcomed me into their light-filled kitchen, where her husband and grown son were waiting. I was still quite broken up, and it was all the easier to cry when among friends.

"What's the hardest thing for you in this?" my friend asked.

Her question cut like a surgeon's knife, instantly exposing my heart. Up came my response, which had long been roiling beneath the surface, now expressed in words for the very first time.

"Why would God give me love for my father, knowing he would end his life this way?"

In other words, wouldn't it have been easier on me if I'd never loved him? Behind this question was the unspeakable one, too awful to utter: *Did God set me up?*

Now then, before you judge me too harshly for having such a horrible thought, let me remind you: I know a setup. I learned it from my mother and I know it with every fiber of my being. I know what it's like to have the rug torn out from under you, making your head spin around to the point that two plus two no longer equals four. I know the setup that leaves you with post-traumatic stress disorder.

"Why would God give me love for my father, knowing he would end his life this way?"

Mother and son spoke nearly in unison, as the prophets of old: "It would have been much worse if you hadn't loved him."

This cut me, too. But this was the startling, shining sword of Truth, and it brought me up short. Worse? It would have been worse?

By God's mercy, I hadn't even known until two days before he died that my father was threatening suicide. Later I discovered he'd purchased a gun and had been promising to use it for six months. In probing into his death, I unearthed so many ugly truths about what was said to him, what was done, what should have been done but wasn't; all the sad details that had added to his despair. But I had really been kept in the dark. I was totally out of the loop, which meant I had no regrets, no remorse, and no heart full of guilt to bear.

God alone brought us our breakthrough on the boat that autumn morning. From the foundation of the world, He chose the means and the moment to give me love again for my father. If He hadn't, I would have believed myself to be part of my father's problem. Instead, God gave me balm for him, as much as his unseasoned heart could receive, and carefully kept me outside the circle of his pain. God gave me the gift of a clean conscience, and He gave it to me five years before, knowing my father would end his life that way.

He is the Rock, his work is perfect:
for all his ways are judgment:
a God of truth and without iniquity,
just and right is he.
Deuteronomy 32:4

Amen.

13

Come In

Let's listen to Clara, speaking as every woman I have visited in a nursing home.

Come in!

I wasn't sleeping, I was just resting. The girls usually make the bed by now, but you can sit there, just move those things over.

Oh, I love the hymns, it doesn't matter, they're all good. You sing your favorite. I haven't sung in years! I used to sing in the choir…takes me right back to West Virginia. We went to church every day in West Virginia. Oh, well, maybe it was Wednesdays and Sundays. My granny took us. Let me think. It was our mother, too, and my brothers and sisters.

No. My father was killed. I remember that day vividly. He went hunting. He was shot, he never came back. I was four years old. Granny came to take care of us. Here's a picture of all of us when we were a family. It's the only one I have. I'm so glad I have that; I can always see what he looked like. I remember that day vividly.

One day, as I reported for my regular music visits at one of my favorite nursing homes, my boss spun her back to me in her swivel chair, like a corporate mogul.

"Come see me when you're done."

Based on bitter experience, I thought I recognized the prelude to my swan song. I figured my hit record was about to fall off the charts.

"Please tell me *now*," I said, pushing her. After three pushes, she confirmed my suspected termination. Budget cuts, she claimed.

That hard young woman had inherited me, as I had her. The turnover for her position was so high that I couldn't remember who had originally hired me, so many directors ago. Maybe it was an achievement that I lasted as long as I did.

Frequent change of staff is typical in the nursing home industry. Once when Chloe and I showed up for work we discovered that the facility had been bought by a new company and the entire staff, from the administrator to the nurse's aides, had been replaced. No one expected us; no one had a record of our previous month's visit for which we hadn't yet been paid. I was only permitted to say hello to a few of my favorite residents that day, without telling them I was really saying goodbye. A few persistent phone calls later, I made the forty-mile drive back to the home to be paid for the previous month—in one-dollar bills from petty cash. Respect can be a hard commodity to come by in life. It's especially hard to find in a nursing home.

What Clara thinks is too often true:

> ...I see lots of people. But they don't see me. The girls come to give me medicine, they make the bed. They check my blood pressure and ask me if I've had a "movement" today. This is where I live, but it's not like my home in West Virginia. I can't even remember how

I got here, I just know I didn't choose it; I would never choose a room like this. It's so small.

We had a big house, and a lot of land. There was always something that needed to be done. We did it all, we were country people, we did things ourselves. Now I can't take a bath or even use the bathroom by myself. I have to sit and wait until someone comes. Look at the bed. It's not even made.

We used to sing. After dinner on Sunday, Mother would play the piano. Oh, little sister, you couldn't sing, but we didn't care, did we? We laughed. We were safe. We were where we belonged. I don't belong here. Everyone is so old. They sit slumped over the table in the dining room. I just eat here in my room. It's too depressing. I had friends, people I grew up with. They're all gone now....

I wouldn't fault any of my bosses just for letting me go. I know there are such things as budget cuts. If that young woman in the swivel chair had shown me some respect, I would have been much more inclined to believe she couldn't afford me. But I think it's safe to say she simply didn't see much value in what I do. The importance a program director assigns to work like mine seems to be directly proportional to the understanding she has for the needs of her residents.

In her defense, my "mogul" boss was never present in the residents' rooms with my dog, guitar, and me. But she was not supposed to be. Such intimate moments were only meant for the one hooked up to the IV, the one in the wheelchair, or the one behind the door, like Clara.

> *I was just thinking about you! I told the nurse, there's a lady from church who comes to see me and she brings her dog. I told her we sing all the hymns together. I haven't been to church in ages, I used to go every day, no, every Wednesday and Sunday, we all went, but my father, he was killed. In West Virginia. I remember that vividly.*

I guess it's human nature. *Jesus did not commit himself unto them, because he knew all men* (John 2:24). I am loved in one facility and despised in the next. Sometimes I'm loved and then despised in the very same facility, before I can catch my breath. One nursing home awarded me "Provider of the Year." But when I went in shortly thereafter to deliver my invoice to my beloved boss I was told, "You know Katherine isn't here anymore, don't you?"

This is why I need a higher motivation to press on. *For ye see your calling, brethren, how that not many wise men after the flesh, not many mighty, not many noble, are called* (1 Corinthians 1:26).

It may sound peculiar to you, or maybe even puffed-up, to say my work is God's calling on my life. Do you remember "Reepicheep," the big, brave mouse in C.S. Lewis's story *Prince Caspian and the Voyage of the Dawn Treader*? He tells of a prophecy spoken over him when he was still in his little mousey cradle, that one day he would see Aslan's Land. Aslan being the Christ figure, as you may recall. And at the story's end, Reepicheep sails into the horizon towards his destiny. I'm not saying I was prophesied over in my wee little bed. But like Reepicheep, you might say my future was predicted, too. Not by a word spoken over me in my cradle, but by an example modeled to me in my sickbed.

When I was three years old, I had pneumonia and nearly died. Apart from the oxygen tent, I can remember very little. But the one thing I've never forgotten is the visit of a stranger. He must have been a patient, just a boy in a plaid flannel bathrobe. He came to my room every day, just to visit me. His attention made me feel important and safe at a time when I was sick and afraid. And after all these years, I remember it vividly.

Nursing homes are a business, and there's no getting around it. But blessedly, the majority of my employers are loving men and women who can feel for the "someones" like Clara.

> ...I'm bored, but there's really nothing I want to do. All my happy memories are about the people. It's the people you miss when everything changes. The ones who know who you are. We did everything together; we laughed at the same jokes. Everything we had we shared; our lives were knitted together like a big blanket that covered us all. Nothing is familiar now.
>
> And I'm not familiar to anyone....

Oh no, dear Clara, you are mistaken. We know who you are.

> Oh, I am so glad you came. I was feeling blue today. I heard you, I heard you outside my door, and I said, "This must be Thursday!" I haven't sung in years! This takes me right back to West Virginia. I told the nurse how you come and we sing the hymns together just like in church. I miss church. We went to church every day in West Virginia. I was just thinking about you. Come in!

14

Natural Causes

It had taken only four years for my friend Michael to completely deplete his hefty inheritance.

Now all his bills were past due, but he was still desperate to find a way to keep spending. Lying to his cousin that he needed money for a home repair, he'd borrowed three thousand dollars which he'd mailed in a brown paper bag to the "Publisher's Clearing House Representative" in Mexico who had promised him a new car in return. Not that he could drive. That was when I received his call.

I didn't ask the Lord if I should get involved. He was drowning, and I just jumped in after him. I'm sure I should have been praying.

Michael was the son of a very dear older friend of mine. While she was alive, he was always in the background, awkward and strange—black knee socks, dress shoes, and shorts. I would try to include him in our conversations, but it felt more like charity than any kind of relationship. When his mother died, I was assured that financially he had "nothing to worry about," and it was all too easy to believe that and leave him to his own devices.

When the bottom fell out, his cousin was too far away and too taxed to step in. I was single and practically around the corner. Plus, I had a rescuer complex, so it was completely in character for me to come running. I think we always tell ourselves we want nothing in return. I guess I wasn't really ready for nothing.

I was amazed, however, and proud of America when I saw the way our system worked for people like Michael.

It wasn't too difficult to get him set up on disability, and I became his Representative Payee. This was not his preference, but I pushed him; how else could he survive? His home was mortgage-free, and now his groceries were provided by food stamps. He had an allowance of a certain amount which miraculously appeared in his checking account every month. And central air conditioning. I confess to you, I was a little envious.

On top of that, the utility companies were forgiving. Yes, the utility companies. Three months of unpaid bills were budgeted into five dollars extra each month, with no interest, accompanied by a new, lower rate. Everyone was so kind, bless America's heart. There was even enough left over to eventually pay back his cousin, who also forgave.

Whenever I tried to coax Michael out of his house, it was like pulling teeth. Back when he was in his early twenties, he had worked for six months, then came home one day without explanation and never returned. That was forty-some years ago. It wasn't good for him to have been hidden in that little home all his life. He never received the medical care that might have helped him.

I eventually managed to take Michael with me to my closest nursing home a couple of times a month. He was in charge of pushing Chloe in her stroller. This made Chloe as nervous as it did me, and I watched him like a hawk, the poor man. But he was comfortable with the residents; after all those years of living with his mother, he seemed practically at home. And he'd had no over-exposure to jade his reactions to people's complaints. If he heard someone crying out from their room, he would abandon Chloe and run in to see what was wrong. He had a heart.

But Michael would always, always lie to me. During our last Christmas visit, upon going upstairs in his home to wash my hands, I saw that one of the bedrooms had been completely emptied of furniture. Everything was gone but the indentations in the carpet. Strangers had come in and bought it all. I grabbed my coat and stormed out, leaving my little gifts and our Wendy's lunch behind.

Whatever his reasons, it was money Michael wanted, and he always wanted more. I knew he'd emptied his mother's jewelry drawer, and now he would be systematically selling the entire contents of the house. I couldn't stop him.

As his payee, I handled his bills. A phone bill came in flying the red flag of a long-distance charge. (He had no provision in his new plan, given his propensity to call Mexico.) When I called the suspicious number, a nice man from a bank answered, informing me that Michael had taken out a reverse mortgage. Since I wasn't his Power of Attorney, I couldn't reverse the reversal. This bank should repent or forever be ashamed of themselves.

Now I was praying. *What should I do?* I called Social Security and explained a "hypothetical" disability and reverse mortgage situation. The woman on the phone was brief and to the point. "Get out now." I appreciated the word. Back we went to the sterile government building and Michael was put in charge of his finances once again. I gave no explanation; I couldn't turn him in. "Can he handle this?" the man behind the counter asked. I didn't think so, but he would have to be a criminal all by himself.

I had always pictured Michael's future in my mind. There he would be, settled in a little government-subsidized nursing home room somewhere in front of a huge TV with all his meals cooked for him, all his needs met. Nothing to entice him because the money was all gone, the source of temptation now fully out of reach. I thought he might be happy that way.

When Michael's mail piled up for days, someone on his block finally called the police. Apparently, an elderly neighbor had gone down to identify the body. His cousin called to tell me the news, with no more explanation for Michael's death than the generic "natural causes."

And so his addiction had come to an end. We bring nothing into this world, and not even a greed as tyrannical as Michael's would allow him to carry anything out.

When I became a Christian intent on pursuing Christian music, I was told I needed a "mission statement," because everyone had one. Wanting to do the appropriate thing, I found Luke 8:39: *Return to thine own house, and show how great things God hath done unto thee.* I chose that Scripture because I could relate to the demoniac. He lived in the tombs, with the dead. No one could bind him; he was driven by the devil to live in the wilderness, all by himself. He was not a people person.

I wasn't either, before Christ. I hid from people; no one could bind me. Driven by my own addictions, I left marriages that were doomed from the start because I was drawn like a magnet to men who would hurt me. My only friends were in the bars; we were all the drinking dead. I did a lot of crying out but wouldn't let anyone near me.

But after Christ came, I was found sitting at his feet, dressed, and in my right mind. I began to see others as made in His image. I began to see them not as the enemy, but as worthy of love. I began to see myself the same way.

Back when Michael sent the money to the PCH scam-man in Mexico, I had called a policeman to meet me at Michael's house because I couldn't convince him he'd been scammed. I thought he might believe the officer. That very patient policeman explained to Michael for nearly an hour before he finally broke down, put his face in his hands and cried, "I'm a fool, I'm a fool!"

I don't have children, but this was, to me, a teachable moment. I put my hand on Michael's shoulder and suggested that he was in a very good place, if he understood himself to be foolish. God had sent His Son to save us from that very thing. God knew we were slaves to our sinful compulsions, and if we did too, then we could run to Him to receive forgiveness and a new, emancipated life.

I had talked often to Michael about the Lord. I prayed for him when I was with him and when I wasn't. But oh-so-sadly, he never came out of the tombs. It's as if that was where he wanted to be.

But the natural man receiveth not
the things of the Spirit of God:
for they are foolishness unto him:
neither can he know them,
because they are spiritually discerned.
1 Corinthians 2:14

15

A Song

Ms. Beatrice lived in one of the poorer nursing homes in the city.

Her building sat on a no-outlet street behind an isolated apartment complex marked by broken windows and safety bars. The only open parking space was usually beside the dumpster.

Once Chloe and I were buzzed in for our regular visits, we would be greeted by the hotel-like lobby. But a few steps beyond the façade, the dismal truth was revealed. Two, sometimes three residents were crowded into each tiny room. Their neglected appearances and lack of personal possessions seemed to cry out, *This is all that's left*. Hope itself had fled the scene, with no one expecting its return.

Ms. Beatrice's room was towards the end of the hall, by the nurse's station. Wearing a washed-out windbreaker over her housecoat and seated in a hard and heavy wooden chair, she would clutch her pocketbook as she waited outside her doorway.

Each week I'd wheel Chloe down the hall and stand in front of her to chat and sing. For months I had been inviting her to sing along, but she never joined me. "I'd rather hear you," she always replied.

Why do you suppose that was?

Was it that we were not on the same level in life, Ms. Beatrice and I? Standing over her, looking down past the expensive purebred dog in the stroller, my attempts to reach her seemed to share an insincerity with the lobby. If I were her, I might not have been inclined to sing with me either. I might have just sat there, watching the show.

Performing is what I know. Before I ever picked up a guitar or walked onto a stage, I learned to perform. As a little girl enmeshed in my mother's distorted reality, I played the role of the perfect child to win her love.

Performing inherently elevates one above the audience—although, ironically, the approval of the audience is what the performer seeks. It's complicated and I have internalized it thoroughly, I'm sorry to say. This sort of perversion of spirit is not eradicated from a person overnight. But years and years of service in Christ can do a girl a world of good.

One day I decided to try something different with my non-singing friend.

"Ms. Beatrice, watch Chloe for a minute?" I grabbed another of those heavy chairs and slid it squeaking down the hall to her side. A small gesture, but one that put us both on the same level.

And then she sang.

It turned out Ms. Beatrice had a beautiful trained voice. She clapped her hands long-ways, up and down, not side to side, and she came to life. We made some noise. Even the nurses looked up from their computers to give Ms. Beatrice the kind of attention she deserved.

"We're having church!" she proclaimed.

"Ms. Beatrice, we are sitting on your front porch now, aren't we? We have been friends for years, and we are just sitting here together watching people go by and singing about the Lord, isn't that right?" The scene flashed through my mind as vividly as if I were remembering instead of imagining it.

"My *girl*friend!" she suddenly said of Chloe, reaching out to pat her head. She hadn't touched her until that day. "That's my *girl*friend!"

One afternoon, Ms. Beatrice threw back her head and took off on her own. I had no idea what to do but follow her, searching for her key, fumbling around on my little nylon string guitar and hoping to support her song.

> *I can't smile by myself*
> *I can't laugh by myself*
> *I can't love by myself*
> *I can't talk by myself*
> *I can't walk by myself*
> *I can't sing by myself....*

She went on for I don't know how long.

"Ms. Beatrice, that was awesome! I've never heard that song before."

"I know...I made it up!" Her face was glowing. "Now you take care of my girlfriend!"

You shall have a song, as in the night when a holy solemnity is kept; and gladness of heart, as when one goes with a pipe to come into the mountain of the LORD, to the mighty One of Israel.
Isaiah 30:29

16

Dear David

Sunday, June 8th

Dear David,

I can't tell you how much it meant to me to spend some time with you last month. I am so very glad I could visit you. I'm sorry that you had to be so sick for me to be prompted to come.

My cousin David was most likely already dying of skin cancer when he called to tell me he was in the hospital. That was April. In late May, I prepared my little camper and Chloe and I went to park in the driveway of his boyhood home which he had now inherited from his parents.

Our visit in your family home was especially comforting to me. I have such happy memories of the time we spent together there when we were growing up.

> *Somehow I was protected from the continual watchings of my mother, and I felt freedom as a child whenever I visited you.*

More like a brother than a cousin, David was just two years older than I. His artistic nature gave us an affinity that I shared with no one else in our family. As kids we would sit with our knees against the big oak bar in their family room and polish off huge bowls of cold shrimp dipped in cocktail sauce. David's mother worked long hours as a waitress, but I thought they were rich.

> *You may not know how safe it made me feel, just to sit beside you on that stool as if we belonged together, in the face of all that "luxury." I love you so much, David.*

His parents, though more sane than mine, had their troubles. His father drank heavily, and after seeing David off to college, had divorced my aunt and remarried. But when David's father was dying, he took his mother (with permission from the new wife) to see him, plopped her down in front of him, and announced that they were now going to forgive each other. They held hands and did so.

> *And I'm so proud of you. You are a lovely and gracious man. Your story of bringing your mother to reconcile with your father was so touching, it made me cry. What a gift you gave them. I wish I could have done something like that for my parents.*

A few days after my father's suicide, I received an anguished call from David. Apparently, during my cousin's final visit with him, my father had openly confessed his plans to end his own life. "I'm so sorry, I should have told you!" David sobbed into the phone. At the memorial service he had read a long and detailed account of their last week together. It was obvious how much he cared.

In contrast to David's tenderness, and despite my pleadings, someone inconceivably insisted that the station wagon in which my father had shot himself be cleaned, overhauled, and used for funeral transport. (I will never understand.) What right did anyone have to drive the vehicle that had served as his grave? To replace broken glass and upholstery as if the devastation could be removed? To put their unfeeling hands on the last precious memory I had of my father sitting behind the wheel, in his old sailor's hat, cautiously driving me to the corner store during our final Thanksgiving visit? He was eighty-nine. It was the last time I saw him before his suicide that Christmas.

The morning of the memorial, I prayed that the Lord would keep me from seeing my father's car in the parking lot. To my relief I didn't notice it on the way in. But as I was leaving, I heard David call over my shoulder, "I'm going to walk Susan out." His arm went around me as he scooped me out of the building. I thought I saw something. "Is that my father's car?" But I was safe under David's arm.

> *I think your wanting your parents to forgive each other is a good picture of what is necessary for all of us. But there is a greater forgiveness that we need. We all need to be forgiven by God for our sins. We have personally broken His laws and offended a Holy God. I wonder if you have ever thought about this.*

There you have it. My not-so-subtle transition.

> *David, my church family is praying for you to be healed of this serious cancer. But we are also praying for you to come to the Lord. David, would you please consider reading the Bible I gave you?*

I'd left him with my big NIV study Bible, the one I'd been given by a friend before I was saved, a friend who was trying to help me just as I was now trying to help David. It was inscribed by the pastor whom God used to bring me to Himself—the man whose cassette teaching tape I had tossed out the window. I hated to part with that Bible, but I was hoping if I gave David something personal, it would mean more to him.

> *I don't know if you've read much of the Bible before, but the Gospel of John might be a great place to start.*

Everyone says that, but I don't know why.

> *The Bible says that "God was reconciling the world to himself in Christ, not counting people's sins against them" (II Corinthians 5:19 NIV). We need forgiveness so we can be reconciled to God. Without faith in Christ, we are estranged from Him, David.*

It's all true, of course, and I shared this letter with my pastor and a friend or two before I mailed it. But maybe I sounded too sure of myself.

> *We never talked about the visit you had from the pastor while you were in the hospital. I don't know how you felt about it.*

That wonderful pastor didn't even know me. I had called his Ohio church from Philly and asked him to go, and he drove forty-five minutes to spend fifteen with David and pray for him. What can we do when someone is dying, besides everything we can think of?

> *I have prayed about writing you this "love letter" (as I am thinking of it). I don't know if I'm saying too much or not enough. But, by His mercy only, I do know the risen Lord Jesus, and I know He calls you to come to Him, David.*
>
> *I don't believe my parents are in heaven. I doubt it very much, because faith in the Lord Jesus changes one's life, and it shows. I talked to my father about the Lord until he told me to "get off his back." Doesn't sound like a transformed heart, does it? This is hard to say, David, but even more than healing from cancer, you (and I) need the cleansing, forgiveness, and perfect goodness of Christ to be given to us. He is the One who brings us to God the Father. Eternal life is freely given to us when we receive the Lord Jesus by faith. You have time, dear cousin. God has given you time. Please—I was going to say please take my words seriously, but it's God's words we must believe.*

All true, completely true. But when you have only so much time or paper, I guess you end up trying to give someone a mini-theology course so you don't miss any details. So you can be sure you've said everything while you still have the chance. I think I was trying too hard. I think I always try too hard.

> *I'm sure you know this famous verse that tells us that God's motive in offering us salvation is His great love: "For God so loved the world, that He gave His only begotten Son, that whosoever believeth in Him should not perish, but have everlasting life" (John 3:16).*
>
> *I don't know all the answers of course, but I have had good teaching. If you have questions and ever want to talk, you could call any time, even in the middle of the night. Or please feel free to just call about anything. I would love to hear from you.*

David's sweet voice. We used to refer to each other as "Relative." "Hello, David, this is your relative calling," and we would laugh. Everyone was so at odds, it was the exception to claim familial ties, much less imply we were happy about it.

He never called, of course—not to talk about God, or anything.

> *As I read what I've written, I remember too well what I used to think of Christians and Christianity before I was saved. I was angry and would have torn up a letter like this. So, I don't know what's in your heart right now. But if I had a cure for cancer, you would want me to tell you. I know of a greater cure, and I am writing to you about Him because I love you.*

I implore you, dear cousin, on Christ's behalf;
be reconciled to God.

With love and hope,
Your "relative,"
Susan

David was a professional artist, a talented and loving man, his work displayed all around the world. From where I'm living now, I would be only fifteen minutes away from him, had he survived.

I think about that all the time.

Now then we are ambassadors for Christ,
as though God did beseech you by us:
we pray you in Christ's stead,
be ye reconciled to God.
II Corinthians 5:20

17

My Little Town

I always assumed I would die in Philadelphia.

That's where I had settled and bought my house after years of being away from home—a home I ran away from, a hometown I hated and vowed I would never return to, and a sad family I chose to leave behind. It was either them or me, and I picked me. As a good, responsible citizen, I was striving to pay off the mortgage before the day of my demise.

I liked Northeast Philadelphia and was thrilled with my row home. It had freshly-refinished hardwood floors and a big front bay window—a real saving grace considering the barren back-alley view. I got to know my neighbors early on and grew to love them. Our street swarmed with children and there were always friendly faces just outside my door. Yes, there was crime around us, but we were a community and looked out for each other. I wasn't lonely there.

I used to say you couldn't pay me to return to my hometown.

> *...Coming home after school*
> *Flying my bike past the gates of the factories*
> *My mom doing laundry*
> *Hanging out shirts in the dirty breeze...*
> –Paul Simon *"My Little Town"*

Turns out, I was the one who had to do the paying; it surely is expensive to move.

It happened so fast. My city taxes went up, took a flying leap up until they were equal to my mortgage. I asked my accountant, and he confirmed the numbers. Suddenly, I didn't think I could afford to stay in my house. I had to do something. Who can pay two mortgages?

During a visit to Ohio a few years earlier, I had taken an impulse detour through my old neighborhood. I was surprised to see how things had changed. The trees had grown so tall. The steel plant had shut down, so the heavy smell of rotten eggs no longer choked the air. The lake, so much cleaner now, boasted a new marina and upscale condos for the boat people to dwell in. It was almost a resort town—or wanted to be.

But the town was not the only thing that had changed. The longer I walked with Christ, the more I felt His promptings to move towards my family instead of away from them. Progress had been made, some of it very pronounced. I had seen the healing of God between my father and myself. But you know, you just can't visit enough. No matter how often you do, you are still a visitor, a guest. And your real home is—well, wherever it is, far away. My two brothers and I were not getting any younger. Our parents were gone, and with my father's suicide we now had a bigger sorrow in common. It seemed the Lord was telling me something.

The idea of returning "home" had occurred to me once after my brother made the casual suggestion, "Why don't you move back? Your family is here." I mentioned it to a friend and quickly dismissed it. "I can't," I told her. "I'll die!"

Well, we all have to die somewhere.

Checking a realtor site online, I was stunned to find the cost of Midwest housing to be less than half of where I was living. I began taking virtual tours of houses and streets and reading up on the safety scores of different areas. Slowly I was closing in on my old neighborhood. Not too close, but wouldn't it be nice to see the school, and the lake, and the railroad tracks?

Trying to think ahead, I considered that maybe a five-year-plan would work. Give me plenty of time to.... well, plan. But the tension of a huge life-change staring me in the face from five years down the road was too consuming for me.

I am a simple person; I can only live one life at a time. And it took only one voice, one friend, during a walk around my Northeast Philly block to ask me, "Why don't you go now?" to relieve me of that burden. Okay. I guess I was ready to go.

Few others were as supportive. My church family was very tiny, and my leaving would create a gaping hole and cut the worship population considerably. When I finally put my house on the market and asked for prayers that it would sell, they kept praying for God to give me patience. At least they did pray with me that God would show me the right house to buy in Ohio—just where He wanted me to be.

On July 13th of that year, yes, I really do remember, I was driving home from my New Jersey nursing home listening to Christmas in July on the radio classics channel. They were playing a half-hour adaptation of *Miracle on 34th Street*. Maybe you recall the movie.

So, the premise is this: Susan, the little radio girl, doesn't believe in Santa. And Kris Kringle, the man everyone thinks is crazy because he believes he *is* Santa, wants to prove his existence to her and make her happy at the same time. Susan wants a new father (divorce) and a house with a white picket fence for Christmas. No small request from such a little girl. But Mr. Kringle comes through at the happy ending of the show. Susan gets her new dad and a little Cape Cod on the edge of town, complete with a white picket fence.

I wasn't even thinking about the program when I came home and opened my computer to the realtor site, my new habit of choice. The night before, in an hour of doubt, I had tried a last-ditch search for anything around Philly that I could possibly afford but came up empty. No encouragement there. Now, when I changed the settings to my hometown, something flashed across the screen. The newest listing of the day, it read: *This is it! Move-in condition, beautiful Cape Cod!*

There it was, on the very street where I grew up. Clicking on the pictures, I found the back yard with the required surround. A Cape Cod, with a white picket fence, for Susan.

I freaked out.

In my expert planning, I was thinking I'd sell my row home, buy a very cheap house with cash, then have a small amount left over to cling to with sweaty hands while I cold-called the local nursing homes for work. But this Cape Cod for Susan, although half the price of my row, would require a mortgage. Who would lend me money in a new state when I had no job?

The man who had helped me with my first mortgage was a brother in the Lord, so I tried him first. Without missing a beat, he said, "I can lend in Ohio."

But then there was that sticky problem of no work. Christ had given me a desire to be responsible; I had paid off a lot of credit card debt after my conversion and my credit rating was good. That was a help. My banker friend thought he could make a case for me if I could give him letters of intent to hire. Time to go visit Ohio. I also had to look at the house.

I made appointments for free trials of my "Music Visits" program with five nursing homes in that general area, packed up Chloe and my little camper and headed for my brother's driveway. "You came all this way to look at only one house?" he asked in disbelief. Staring back at him from the brink of yet another major life-transition, I was too nervous to even try to explain.

Fear notwithstanding, all five nursing home trials went very well, and every activities director wrote me a glowing letter of intent. The Lord was working, and it was showing. I told Him, *Unless I hate it, Lord, I'll buy this house.*

Along with the realtor, a long-lost cousin and his wife stood waiting in the driveway for the look-see. He was very encouraging. It was quite a feeling to have family helping me. It was quite a feeling to have family at all.

Honestly, if I'd known how difficult the whole thing was going to be, I may never have done it. But the Lord was going before me, and He doesn't tell us what we "can't bear now" (John 16:12). With all the aspirations of the ignorant, I stuffed what the DIY movers had left behind into my tiny camper and set my face for Ohio. After finally signing all the papers and burning holes in the fenders from overloading the camper, Chloe and I came squealing safely up our driveway at nine-thirty that night. The tires gave the fenders little mohawks, but praise God nothing went flat.

My new kitchen greeted me with a gap-toothed grin. No refrigerator, no stove. The basement was just as happy. No washer, no dryer. The former owner had missed or mistaken the homeowner's warranty he paid for and thought somehow it applied to his own appliances. So, some little glitches. We had arrived.

Not long after, my brother called me from the sandwich shop beside the local Style Mart Salon. Laughing, he said it was his regular Saturday night hang out. The following Saturday I timed my haircut for five-thirty and bumped into him on my way out. (He didn't know I'd prayed him there.) "Hey! Have you eaten?"

Driving home I considered that "chance" meetings like this could never have happened if I hadn't moved back. It was one of many hopeful signs. But it was too soon to tell if the investment of myself would make the difference I'd prayed for in healing my remaining family relationships. Though the Lord had clearly brought me back, all I could be certain of in my radical obedience to Him was my good faith attempt at building a bridge that spanned my lifetime. It remained to be seen if anyone would cross over to meet me.

And the LORD shall guide thee continually, and satisfy thy soul in drought, and make fat thy bones: and thou shalt be like a watered garden, and like a spring of water, whose waters fail not. And they that shall be of thee shall build the old waste places: thou shalt raise up the foundations of many generations; and thou shalt be called, The repairer of the breach, The restorer of paths to dwell in.
Isaiah 58:11-12

18

Get Well Soon

The urgent care doctor took one look at my swollen knees and hands the size of baseball mitts and sent me hobbling straight out the door to the nearest emergency room.

The emergency room doctor saw beyond my swelling to the red streaks advancing up my arm and went straight to the phone. "We don't know if this is an infection or an auto-immune reaction and we are not equipped to find out," he reported.

Returning to me, he took out his black magic marker to record the progression of the streaks and ambulanced me to the supposedly superior city hospital. There I spent an eight-day fun-filled staycation being pumped full of big-gun antibiotics and that notorious inflammation fighter, king prednisone.

During my unscripted eight-day tenure, my symptoms mystified the doctors. They tested me for everything and found nothing. A medical, rheumatological, and surgical team attended my bedside every morning. Busily probing my distorted knees and hands, they discussed my body parts without discerning the owner. I of course claimed title, even in that condition.

My nurse came to tell me I had no veins (meaning she couldn't find them) and it was time for me to have a PICC line.

Do you know what a PICC line is? I hope not. But I will tell you, the acronym stands for "peripherally inserted central catheter."

Ugh.

Every time she said it, she held out her forefingers a good foot apart. *Tell me it's not that long.*

"Do you have to keep doing that?" I complained.

"You don't want me to lie to you, do you?"

The big day brought a small woman in a shower cap barely visible behind a cart full of equipment. I glanced down at the poor little IV clinging pathetically to my right hand. I felt sorry for it. I decided it could stay.

"No, thank you!" I called.

"No?" she asked.

I was full of power. "No, I don't want it, I'm fine." Wonder of wonders, there was no argument, and off she went.

In came my nurse. "Where did she go?"

"I sent her away," I replied as queen.

"You what? Listen . . ."

And she explained so kindly, that even though it was really her fault that she couldn't find my perfectly sound veins (she didn't say that), the dying little IV in my hand would not last the weekend. The PICC line nurses didn't work on weekends, and I would be up a creek if I didn't get this taken care of now. It made much more medical sense to pump the heavier meds into the heartier vein. She stopped short of mentioning her presidency over the debating club at nursing school because, sadly, she'd made her point.

She hunted down the little shower cap gal and warned me of her return later in the day. But in the afternoon, someone else appeared. A quiet woman with big brown eyes.

"I'm Diane; I'm the PICC line nurse." She saw little Hermie. "He's cute!"

Yes, he was.

"Hermie" was a marshmallow snowman who was playing guitar with his stick arms and hands while standing on a chocolate-covered graham cracker. My pastor's wife had given him to me as an early Christmas gift. I took great inspiration from him since my own hands were too puffed-up to play at all. He managed so well with just his little sticks, bless his heart.

"I play guitar," I explained, in case she couldn't guess by looking at my hands.

"You do? I love guitar! Do you play for services?" Her lovely eyes grew wide.

As her rattling cart swung towards my bed, I noticed a little Christian fish taped to the top shelf.

"Is that an ichthys?" I asked.

"No . . ."

"Isn't that the Christian fish?" I asked again.

"Oh, yes, I thought you said 'necklace'!" She was so cute.

"Are you a Christian?" Of course she was.

"Oh, yes!" And that was it. The two of us locked hearts as if we'd been friends for years.

Diane was single too, and she was lonely. She struggled to fit in at church because everything was all about families and couples. The shower cap woman I'd turned away was someone Diane had personally trained and taught everything she knew. But now that woman laughed at Diane behind her back and treated her spitefully. The whole department had turned against her. It all hurt so much; she didn't know what to do.

I barely noticed the dreaded procedure, except for some pain. But since I trusted my sister, the time flew by. Diane worked seamlessly while we laughed and shared. Then we gently held hands and prayed for each other. She prayed so sweetly for my condition, and I for her loneliness and nasty situation at work. Before she left, Diane sat down beside me and played a YouTube video of "I Must Tell Jesus," an old hymn her mother used to love.

I must tell Jesus all of my trials;
I cannot bear these burdens alone;
In my distress He kindly will help me;
He ever loves and cares for His own.
–E. A. Hoffman, 1894

Almost to the door, she turned around. "You don't know how much this has meant to me. I have been so discouraged. I needed this so much." We were both teary-eyed, and she was gone.

And is this the manner of man, O Lord GOD? (II Samuel 7:19 KJV)
Do you deal with everyone this way, O Sovereign LORD? (II Samuel 7:19 NLT)

We can run, baby, or we can hobble, but where will we go from His presence? We can make our beds in hell or in hospital, and behold, God is there. We can take the wings of the ambulance and be rushed to the uttermost parts of the city, and even there, His right hand will hold us.

Who comforteth us in all our tribulation, that we may be able to comfort them which are in any trouble, by the comfort wherewith we ourselves are comforted of God (II Corinthians 1:4).

Once I discovered I wasn't going to die, my priority after being thrown into the hospital was to get myself thrown out. Especially since I had a little someone waiting for me at home. Having been whisked away so quickly, I never even got to say goodbye to Chloe, my security blanket. I'd fed her, pottied her, left her in her crate, and rushed out the door. Since then, my dear neighbors had been taking care of her.

Chloe is not certified as an emotional-support dog. That's only because in order to do so, I'd have to "certify" myself as well. I know I qualify, but I'd rather not make official what everyone probably knows already.

But if you'd ever buried your nose in her neck and smelled fresh baby shampoo, if you'd ever watched the shadows of her long ears swing while walking her on a sunny day, or if you'd ever been tossed into the hospital without her, you might understand my dependency. Especially following my mid-week stay-cation PTSD melt-down which we will now explore.

I was diagnosed in my late twenties by the therapist who basically saved my life.

At first, he saw me for ten dollars a session so I could come five days a week. His ambition was to re-raise me. Years of my mother's controlling scrutiny had distorted my perception to the point that I couldn't pump gas or go into a department store without believing every eye was upon me. I was barely functioning. He was my only friend. I wasn't capable of having any others.

Post-Traumatic Stress Disorder can misrepresent any relationship. If a situation with your friend triggers the memory of your trauma, suddenly you don't "see" your friend anymore. She looks or sounds like your enemy. Soldiers bring it back with them from the war.

That's because, by definition, PTSD is no respecter of situations. It will intrude its nasty little self wherever it wants: at church, at work, or right in the middle of one's bliss-filled hospital holiday.

Halfway through my particular eight days of happiness, someone had written on my whiteboard that I had a possible departure date of tomorrow. *Tomorrow!* I was filled with clawing, grasping hope. I questioned the morning intern. He said he hadn't heard and left to talk to the two nurses outside my door. I was leaning as far forward in the bed as I could, practicing ESP to see if I could figure out what they were saying. *Oh, please let me out of here.*

In a burst of confidence I called out, "Hey, can you come in here and talk about me? Can I hear it, too?" I repositioned my face into a perfect smile of desperation.

The two nurses came in and announced that it was unorthodox to have their morning report in front of the patient. I tried to explain about the going home possibility and the propriety of understanding my own care.

Something went terribly wrong in our communication. The night nurse had a flat look on her face and an even flatter sound to her voice. Unsmiling, she spoke my name in a certain tone. I sensed a deep disapproval. Bold and unguarded, I had spoken up, stood up for myself, thinking I deserved information. Now I was at the mercy of this woman. Suddenly there was a shifting, a shame, a coldness; I felt ice breaking and falling on me from the ceiling. Awful forebodings. My childhood.

It's amazing how crying uncontrollably in front of most adults will immediately cause you to lose your credibility. I saw them exchange glances. The harder I tried to stop, the deeper the shame. It was hopeless.

The "offending" night nurse came back to me later in the day. She sat down and we talked. By then I could at least give some impression of composure. I shared enough to help her understand, but no more. (I don't have to tell people everything, I am just telling you.) We worked it out and she left on a positive note.

Blessedly, that kind of flashback doesn't happen very often anymore. And I can usually tell by the overwhelming strength of my emotions that I'm caught in the throes of a PT reaction. But discernment is necessary, because even if intense, my feelings are often appropriate. I was never allowed to have needs or stand up for myself as a child. With Christ as my teacher, I am learning now.

I once found an article addressing PTSD from a Biblical perspective. It suggested that reading Scripture actually rewires our minds. Kind of like being "re-raised." Anyone in Christ is bound to Him by His living Spirit who never tires of changing us from glory to glory. Our Father is working, and Christ is working, to this very day (John 5:17). It is God's purpose to make us grow, and grow we will. Even if you, like me, received a childhood full of bad information.

But we all, with open face beholding as in a glass the glory of the Lord, are changed into the same image from glory to glory, even as by the Spirit of the Lord (II Corinthians 3:18).

The morning after my melt-down I received a text from a friend at church. "Would it be okay if I brought Chloe to see you today?"

Okay? I burst into convulsive sobs.

My friend worked with her own dogs in Canines for Christ and presented herself in an enviably professional manner. That, and the mention of "therapy," and she was speaking the language of the hospital. The gates swung open for Miss Chloe in her dog stroller, no questions asked.

I was so excited I was sitting up in a chair.

In she wheeled, and when Chloe realized it was me, she cried and trembled violently. I practically crawled into the stroller to comfort her. Five minutes later she was stretched out, sound asleep.

"That's the most relaxed she's been," my friend observed. That made two of us.

By the arrival of the eighth day, I had finally worn out my welcome at the hospital.

"I'm surprised they didn't throw you out before this," quipped my nurse when she learned I had no health insurance. Apparently the Hippocratic Oath had prevailed because they let me stay until my hands and knees had turned into usable body parts again.

Providentially, months before my illness, my friend Myriam had arranged to visit me on what ended up being the night before my release.

After seven days of solitude, Chloe was overjoyed to see her. Myriam picked up my keys from my neighbors to relieve them from "Chloe duty," and she and my little girl bedded down in my guest room for the night. The next day Myriam drove to the hospital to spring me.

Eight days of heavy meds had effectively microwaved my insides. As soon as I had signed the release forms, I became violently ill and locked myself in the bathroom for hours, hiding my symptoms so that no one could stop me from going home. When Myriam arrived, I threw on the clothes I'd been ambulanced in, plastered a smile on my face, and leaning heavily on Myriam's arm, tried not to meet anyone's eye while she smuggled me onto the elevator and out the door.

I was never so happy to see a humble little living room full of Goodwill furniture in my life. I sank to the floor and held Chloe for a long time until I realized I couldn't get up, and Myriam helped me onto the sofa. There I stayed for a week while she nursed me back to some semblance of health.

Since my symptoms had stumped modern medicine, my family doctor wanted to give me a new career as a professional patient, announcing, "There are always more tests!" But by the time Myriam went home, I had shrunk to my original size and could walk, keep food down, and play my instrument. I decided one career was enough for me and I would like to return to mine, thank you. While I was in the hospital, I wasn't sure that would even be possible. I didn't know if I would ever get my life back again. But God is so kind. A few weeks later, although one of us was still quite pale, Chloe and I went back to work.

Never mind the darkness, it's bright as light. Never mind the mystery, He sees the secrets. All things are manifest to the God who is the health of our countenance and the restorer of our souls. He has promised His children that goodness and mercy shall follow us all the days of our lives.

And there's nothing anyone can do about it.

A BLESSING IS IN IT

The LORD will preserve him and keep him alive;
and he shall be blessed upon the earth...
The LORD will strengthen him upon the bed of languishing:
thou wilt make all his bed in sickness.
Psalms 41: 2-3

19

Lunch

I've known my older friend Mary since the day I was born. She has aged considerably since then, but I, apparently, am still ten years old.

Condescension aside, Mary invited me to lunch, presumably to celebrate my release from the hospital. Having survived one ordeal, I felt empowered to brave another. So I accepted. How bad could it be?

My cell phone rang just as we sat down. It was the ambulance company returning my inquiry regarding financial assistance.

I never should have mentioned my medical bills to Mary, or how they would be paid by my Christian Health Sharing Network. Blessedly, the ambulance folks on the phone agreed to give me a discount of four thousand dollars. That kind of break was unheard of, according to an alarmist in my family who had previously counseled me to anticipate bankruptcy. So I hung up with a smile on my face and turned to Mary to explain.

Never explain.

"Well, maybe now you'll get a job!" Mary said, wagging her head.

"What am I doing now?"

"I mean a real job, with health benefits." She is tough.

"Mary, do you know how valuable my work is to me?"

"So is paying your bills!"

How old am I? Well, no point arguing.

Mary does not value me. I imagine she thinks she loves me, but I am not a success in her eyes. To her, success is good deeds, an excellent income, and the pride associated with both. I trust I have these good deeds, because my Savior has ordained that I should walk in them. But my tax return won't register my true riches. And unfortunately for Mary, she doesn't see them.

Despite our rough beginning, lunch was lighthearted. I tried to show love to Mary, listen with a caring heart, and encourage her in everything she said that I could possibly agree with. I prayed a blessing silently to myself and said nary a word about the LORD, as she has told me more than once that I say too much about Him and people don't like to be told.

I was putting on my coat. I don't know how it happened.

"So and So is such and such and his family has turned him away, and his church has turned him away, so we are his family now, and he is a lovely man, and he is WELCOMED in OUR church," Mary announced.

I said nothing.

"What do YOU think about people who are such and such?" she persisted.

I could hardly zip my coat. Two zippers. I was having trouble. I had been praying for an opportunity to witness; now, I was praying for help. I stuttered as I answered.

"W-w-we as Christians are to believe what God says about such and such—"

"Oh, no, I don't believe it! I don't believe God says hateful things about turning people out of the church!" I ducked as her rebuttal whistled by my head.

"Well, wait," I reasoned, "the goal is not to turn people out of the church. God really wants them to come *to* Him and the church, but He wants them to turn away from sin, like we all must do, just like you and I—"

"I don't have much sin," she interrupted. "I haven't done many bad things."

How old is she?

"But Mary, God is Holy, we need to be forgiven and cleansed by Jesus."

"These people aren't doing anything wrong. They were born that way. I don't believe God says those hateful things. I am very lenient. I knew what you thought before I asked you. I could tell by the look on your face."

I told you she's tough.

She turned her face very firmly up to me and declared, "I am very nice."

I see. Nicer than God, apparently, Mary. That could be a problem.

Think not that I am come to send peace on earth: I came not to send peace, but a sword. For I am come to set a man at variance against his father, and the daughter against her mother, and the daughter in law against her mother-in-law. And a man's foes shall be they of his own household.

Matthew 10:34-36

20
God Will Take Care of You

I suppose it is the vanity of our youth that fools most of us into believing we will always retain our vigor. But when the keepers of the house begin to tremble, fears we never even imagined can rise up against us in force. They seem to derive their satanic strength from sucking the very lifeblood out of our perishing outward man.

In self-defense and to succor my own soul, in the following three stories I will face my demons, hoping to subdue them by my experiences and the sure promises of God. I have been young and now am (nearly) old, yet I have never seen the righteous forsaken. When the work outlives the worker, when creativity gives way to confusion, when the singer forgets her song, God is faithful. Even when we can't remember ourselves, God will remember us.

The Mighty

Mr. Saunders was a large, imposing Lutheran man who had built his home with his own two hands. And this was no log cabin.

I don't mean to slight log cabins, and I know there are some gorgeous ones. My point is only that this dwelling-place was not rustically homemade. It looked like something from right off the rack at Macy's, if I may switch similes. It was an amazing life achievement, of which any man would be forever proud. Mr. Saunders raised his considerable family there, under the authority of Christ and himself. He could be intimidating, but his children knew he loved them.

When his daughter Katy brought Chloe and me to meet him, Mr. Saunders had just taken his first step down from independent to assisted living. Facilities such as the one he was in offer increased care levels to accommodate the progression of disease as well as the "natural" decline of aging. Whatever the case for Mr. Saunders, this was not a happy step.

Nevertheless, as I sang a hymn for him he harmonized with me, and as a former player, held my guitar to see what his big hands could still do. Then Katy pulled out the photo album of the building of their house, and the three of us went through it, page by page. I was struck by the sad irony that something so beautiful and well-made would long survive the builder himself. *(What profit hath a man of all his labor which he taketh under the sun?)* After closing the album, Mr. Saunders leaned back in his chair and closed his eyes while Katy told of his Sunday school superintendence, eldership, songwriting, poetry, his son the pastor, his many witnessing methods for the Lord.

By the time Mr. Saunders landed in skilled care, he was placed where I worked and I could now visit him "on the clock." No longer able to even lift those mighty hands to answer the phone when Katy called, he was most understandably discouraged. But I came prepared by God Himself, who is not unrighteous to forget our labors of love. Neither would He let Mr. Saunders forget.

"Hi, Mr. Saunders, it's Susan and Chloe. I'm Katy's friend. I met you in your last apartment. I'm so glad to see you today! I know you're not much of a dog-person, but we both wanted to say hello. How are you?"

His was not an enthusiastic reply.

I continued. "I remember when we saw you last, you told me all about the way you yourself built your very own home...." I began pulling the memories of his many accomplishments out of my pockets, out of the drawers, off the walls—simply blanketing his bedclothes with one metaphorical medal after another, until he lay there like the decorated soldier-for-Christ that he was. He was smiling.

Now, this was for him from the Lord, no doubt. But I was the one covered with Holy Spirit goosebumps and filled with joy. (I have no Biblical defense for Holy Spirit goosebumps. You may take my word, or not, in Christian liberty.)

Not long after that, the Lord took Mr. Saunders home. Blessedly, in the few months I had known him, I had been primed by God and privileged to be a messenger of encouragement.

But sometimes I encounter situations for which I am not so well equipped.

The Clever

On the secured memory care units where Chloe and I spend many hours, I can usually enter quickly into someone else's world. Wherever the conversation goes, I will happily follow. And I am usually a good judge of whether a resident can handle something like giving Chloe one of her treats.

Once, however, I was mistaken when a woman I'd just met took the dog treat and immediately raised it to her own mouth. I jumped to pull it back down, but as soon as I let go, her hand flew back up to her own mouth. Repeat.

"You can't eat that, it's dog food!" I burst out, resorting to the very direct approach. She glared at me with contempt. "I wasn't going to *eat* it; I was going to give it to her from my *mouth*."

I suddenly imagined her former occupation, as if she'd toured the world working with trained seals in the circus. I had to admit, although she clearly thought I was an idiot, her idea was very clever. Somewhere, deep in the damaged workings of her mind, a shred of ingenuity had remained.

I confess to you now, my secret fear, because you won't tell anyone. What if one day I too, have nothing left but my ingenuity?

Unlike Mr. Saunders, I'll have no photo album to serve as witness to the life achievements of which I am so proud.

I shall be at the memory care door, ready to leave, asking the aide for the code, but this time she won't tell me. With her very patient voice, she'll turn me around and redirect me, "Let's go this way for a while." And I will follow her, pushing the stuffed dog that I think is Chloe in my toy stroller, resuming my "ministering" work to those who smile at me as I play an invisible guitar. ("I think she's playing guitar, she used to sing in nursing homes," the staff will whisper.) This is a terrible fear. I'm not so sure I should have written it down.

I have sung at the bedsides of dying saints and sinners, witnessing firsthand the ravages of the curse upon their bodies and minds. But when I fail, who will sing to me? No daughter as dear as my friend Katy will testify to my good works, given to me by God to bless my days. If my creativity betrays me with confusion, who will be there to remind me of who I am?

And even to your old age I am he; and even to hoar hairs will I carry you: I have made, and I will bear; even I will carry, and will deliver you (Isaiah 46:4).

Even when we can't remember ourselves, God will remember us.

The Fragile

Every other month Chloe and I spend a long Saturday afternoon in a large, upscale, locked memory unit. We go up and down the wide, open halls; stopping to visit and sing to anyone we meet, from little impromptu groups to individuals who don't like to come out of their rooms. We are all instantly old friends. The whole happy affair culminates in a half-hour sing-along at one far-side of the unit, often padded with folks from the other far-side who have followed us there; "I'm coming after you, you won't get rid of me so easily!"

On this day, a (very patient) aide brought in a woman without shoes, who could no longer navigate even sitting in a chair without much direction and help. "She won't stay, she likes to roam," I was advised. Wondrously, upon sitting, the resident decided to stay. Since I report to my boss the specifics of the day's visits, I took names from everyone before the music started. This was a tender subject, this name-remembering, and needed to be handled with care. We were doing fine until I came to the woman without the shoes. She couldn't tell me her name. Passing lightly over her, I completed the list and almost all of us began to sing. Still sitting quietly and comforted by the happy, familiar songs, our shoeless friend's face was now glowing. I paused for a moment to approach her. Touching her arm and leaning down I gently offered, "I wonder if you would tell me your name."

"Roberta," she said, smiling up at me.

Be not dismayed whate'er betide,
God will take care of you;
Beneath his wings of love abide,
God will take care of you.

God will take care of you,
Through ev'ry day,
O'er all the way;
He will take care of you,
God will take care of you.
–Civilla D. Martin, *1905*

21
Mother's Day

"How was your Mother's Day?" the clerk at the drugstore inquired.

"Traumatic. Just awful."

He gave me the thumbs up sign and then realized what I had answered. We let it go at that.

While my mother was living, I hated this holiday because shopping for a card was such a miserable business. No matter how long I combed through the Hallmark display, I couldn't find one that told the truth. I didn't want to lie and thank her for the loving way she'd cared for me and taught me about the important things in life. I always ended up with the plainest card I could find, and then felt guilty sending it.

Nowadays, I rarely think of my mother, or think of myself as childless. But when the second Sunday of May arrives each year, I am forced to remember both.

My pastor does not preach Mother's Day sermons, and I thank God for that. It's not as if it's a biblical celebration. Nevertheless, on this particular Mother's Day, I seemed to be surrounded by babies, all clutched in the bosoms of their mothers as they practically fell over me to congratulate each other in the pew. This was followed by the awkward moment of afterthought as they turned to wish me a "good week." (Translation: *You're childless and have no family of your own so that's the best we can do.*) At the risk of repeating myself, it was a very tearful day.

But every family harbors its own pain. There's pain if you have a family, and pain if you don't. And Satan, the father of lies, takes our pain and turns it into the Viking-barbed life-piercing club of shame, beating us without mercy until we believe we are to blame for it all, just because of who we are.

I am sensitive. My accuser says, "Too sensitive." It's both a problem and one of my greatest blessings. Surely, one cannot be involved in any art form without it. And in my nursing home work, I am reminded, and often, to be grateful for the way I am wired, for any loneliness and heartbreak I've experienced.

Arriving at Margaret's room in assisted living, I had found her sitting on her rolling seat-walker two inches away from her TV screen, with the volume blaring. Once I got her attention, she pushed herself away from the noise, cooing as she bent to kiss the top of Chloe's head.

"Oh, you sweet thing, did you come to see me?"

Noticing some newly arrived flowers on her dresser, I made a careful inquiry, stepping around the specifics of Mother's Day. It's risky to mention any holiday to an isolated nursing home resident. "They're from my son," she answered, chirping over Chloe like a little bird.

"Oh, you have a son?" I proceeded, feeling encouraged for her.

"Yes…I had two sons. One committed suicide. I was the one who found him." Her childish tone had changed, but she was still addressing Chloe. She had yet to speak directly to me.

My encouraging notions fled. "Oh, Margaret (touching her arm), I am so very sorry. We had a suicide in our family, too."

"Did you?" I could hear an undertone of hope in her voice as she looked up at me, suddenly recognizing what we shared. I had offered my sorrow to Margaret, not to burden her, but to join her, and she had accepted it. We were now companions in our common grief, connected by an intimacy that can only be earned.

In much the same way, the Lord Jesus, our Faithful High Priest, is able to sympathize with our weaknesses—having been tempted, having learned obedience, having carried our sorrows. Our God earned the way to our hearts through his own pain. I trust you understand my paraphrasing.

Time and again, this is my comfort. And whenever I blame myself for being single, I can think of Him. Someone, not a thoughtful person, once told me, "I couldn't imagine you married. You're too much you." No. Jesus is the only One who's too much Himself. There is absolutely no one like Him at all. And there's not a drop of shame in His being only-begotten. There's only glory.

But shame is an obscenely resilient opponent, a rat terrier clamped to the bone of your shoulder. You get used to walking around with him. He weighs a ton, but you grow accustomed to stooping. You blush when you needn't. When the security alarm goes off as you leave the store, you wonder if there might just be something in your bag that you haven't paid for. And God help you if a policeman is behind you in traffic.

But again, our dear Lord not only removed our shame, he despised it. As He killed death by dying, He shamed the shame itself. He sent that little rat dog running and yelping away, forever loosing his hold on anyone in Christ. I need to remember that when my accuser reproaches me for who I am: motherless, childless, single—and bought with the very blood of God.

...neither let the eunuch say, Behold, I am a dry tree. For thus saith the LORD unto the eunuchs that keep my sabbaths, and choose the things that please me, and take hold of my covenant; Even unto them will I give in mine house and within my walls a place and a name better than of sons and of daughters: I will give them an everlasting name, that shall not be cut off.
Isaiah 56:3b-5

22

From Faith to Faith

*Now faith is the substance of things hoped for,
the evidence of things not seen.*
Hebrews 11:1

The Bible never describes faith as a leap that would leave us hanging in midair. When trouble comes, God knows we need a firmer foundation than that.

My Chloe has a gallbladder issue which manifests itself in various frightening ways. But as any hyper-vigilant dog mother will tell you, you get to know the signs. So during one particular flare-up, when I hurried her to the animal clinic, I expected the usual diagnosis, obtained by the usual ultrasound.

The waiting room was crowded and the young vet on duty was flustered. I could tell she wasn't keen on taking the time for an extensive test, but I pushed just the same.

Ten minutes later, full of sympathies, she called me into the little exam room.

"I'm sorry, I'm so sorry, but Chloe has advanced liver cancer. It's in all six lobes of her liver, there's nothing we can do." She proceeded to draw me a picture of something that looked like a splayed cow's udder, scratching in all the segments with her pen. I was devastated.

In situations like this, I run to my Bible and ask the Lord for a verse. I found Hebrews 11 and decided to take the whole chapter of faith for myself. But it was verse 35 that leapt off the page and into my heart: *Women received their dead raised to life again* (Hebrews 11:35). God has such a history of kindnesses to women. I took this as encouragement to pray for healing. Another friend prayed that it wouldn't be cancer at all.

Emboldened by my verse, I decided to ask for a repeat ultrasound, this time with the older and wiser owner of the clinic. He scheduled it for the next afternoon.

After working an endless nursing home hour without her, I was on my way to the clinic to pick Chloe up when another verse came to my mind: *Do you believe I am able to do this?* (Matthew 9:29).

I didn't know what I was supposed to believe, but as I walked in the door, I hoped with all my heart that I believed it.

"You've come to get your baby?" The receptionist's voice had a hopeful ring. A side door opened and the smiling vet appeared.

"Come on back! I have good news for you. I see no evidence of liver cancer. Here, I'll show you."

Little Chloe lay on her back inside the padded tube, one assistant at her head and one at her feet, like the angels who stood guard in the empty tomb. Moving his magic wand on Chloe's belly, the doctor pointed to the monitor.

"See that? That's all good liver. Now see this? That's her gallbladder, full of sludge."

Crying and milking his hand, I announced to the entire office, "We've been praying! We've all been praying!"

I couldn't wait to tell everyone the good news. Starting at the top, I called an elder brother in the Lord and sounded my trumpet.

"Chloe does not have liver cancer! The vet did a second ultrasound and her liver is fine, it's just her gallbladder! She's going to be okay!" I took a breath and listened for his rejoicing.

He was practically speechless. "Oh...well, that's good news," he muttered. "I don't understand what happened, though."

Since when do we understand everything?

But not every elder brother has been so reluctant to believe. The late and great George Müller gave us a tremendous example of a Christian living at the peak of faith. With utter dependence upon God's provision, he never asked for money to fund his orphanage in England. God moved saint after saint to invest in his Kingdom work. I was halfway through his biography when I was inspired to plant some "seed money" of my own.

At the time I was renting an apartment in an old house in Philly, with 250,000 miles on my Honda and two thousand dollars to my name. My mechanic assured me the car was fine, but he must have meant it would be fine for him, who, if experiencing a break-down in the dark on some country road all by himself, would be able to lift the hood and fix something. But my budget did not allow for car payments.

Then I learned that a missionary on the other side of the globe was praying for a motorcycle. Transportation for transportation became my bargaining prayer. *Lord, I cannot afford to save for a car, so I will spend for one, as an investment, and buy the man his bike.* I was full of joy writing the check. I was under no compulsion; I believed the same Lord that had led Mr. Müller was leading me.

The following week, during one of our brief and awkward phone conversations, my mother asked me, "Did you get my letter?"

"No," I answered, my stomach churning at the thought.

At 4:00 p.m. the next day, the mailman knocked with a registered letter, requesting my signature. Inside the envelope was a check for $10,000. CDs my mother had bought for her children long ago had matured. She knew nothing of my need for a car.

In the morning I went straight to the dealership, where I immediately explained to the nice salesman, "Look at me! Do I look like a person who can pay cash for a car? God did this for me!" (I never seem to impress anyone; I don't know why I always try.) "Phoebe," who I named after the servant of the church in Romans 16:1, was a bubble-shaped black Yaris stick-shift. She bravely was the first to tow my little camper. "I think you're crazy," my mechanic announced. Never mind.

One of George Müller's favorite verses was Hebrews 13:8, *Jesus Christ the same yesterday, today and forever*. He lived to show that the God who did wonders in the Old Testament was the same God who still does wonders today. But our brother George didn't just appreciate the verse. He believed it.

What are we afraid of? Do we think it honors Christ to compartmentalize His living water into the freezer trays of our limited minds, and only portion it out one hard little cube at a time? Do we think that makes His mysteries easier to swallow? I'm sorry; I'm too thirsty for that. I'm with George.

Some would say that human error misdiagnosed Chloe's cancer. Or was it God who either healed or suppressed her disease, giving us more years of ministry and joy instead of the heartbreakingly small window we were originally offered? George Müller could have been a good businessman who knew how to charm people into supporting him. Or did God in His faithfulness supply his orphans' every need?

A famous (dead) scientist once said, "There is no god. No one directs the universe." A more famous (resurrected) Christ once said, *Thrust your hand into my side, and be not faithless, but believing* (John 20:27). I have no time for the dreams of dead men.

I'm sorry, I'm too impatient for that. I'm with Christ. He is the LORD, He changes not, yesterday, today and forever.

*But without faith it is impossible to please him:
for he that cometh to God must believe that he is,
and that he is a rewarder of them that diligently seek him.*
Hebrews 11:6

23

Tribute

*Precious in the sight of the Lord
is the death of his saints.*
Psalms 116:15

It was an unexpectedly eventful trip.

Between my camper, my guitar, mini-sound system, CDs, and Chloe, we constituted a heavy load on my little Volkswagen. No wonder the right brake seized up as we were winding, then screeching our way through the hills of Lancaster County, Pennsylvania.

By God's grace and my sheer desperation, we made it to the campground. Plans were shifted but not halted. I would still be able to sing at the sweet country church that had invited us, if I could just find somebody to repair my poor sagging car in time.

After trying five different repair shops, I was parked in the driveway of a school staring at my phone when a woman pulled up next to me.

"Are you looking for something?" she asked.

I babbled. Visiting from Ohio, brake seized, staying in a campground, invited to sing in a little church, tried five repair shops, etc., etc. Needed to drive home on Sunday so I could work on Monday, etc., etc.

"Oh. Go to the Ford dealer. They're great, they're right up the street." She pointed over her shoulder.

I don't know about great, but they temporarily "fixed" (it only *cost* enough to be permanent) the problem so I could sing at the church and get home again. And happily, I could still squeeze in dinner with my friends Ann and Boyd who lived just a few miles from the campground.

You have met these beloved saints, but not by name. They were among the famous "deluded" ones who believed in being born again back when I "knew" being born again was a hoax. I was in their Bible study, learning about Christ before I could stammer His Name. They have always shown above-and-beyond kindness to me.

My dearest Ann, now departed, was the embodiment of generosity. She and Boyd were the first to invite both Chloe and me to dinner. I didn't know dogs could be included as invited guests. She would overfeed me, and Chloe too, if I'd let her, ladening me with gifts upon every departure. Vitamins, water bottles, sandwiches, yogurts, coffee; items would fly out of her cupboards. "These are those throwaway spoons," she'd say, head down, going through the bag she had packed for me. Not to mention the many gifts of money. (I've always imagined Boyd frantically waving his arms in the other room as Ann offered to give me more and more. *"Boyd, take Susan's car to the station and fill it up with gas!" "Dear, dear,"* he'd say, his face losing color. Of course I am teasing. Boyd was every bit as giving as Ann. She really had asked him to fill up my car, but I managed to prevent it.)

Ann appreciated every good thing about people. I always thought she was too self-deprecating because she was such an intelligent woman with so many gifts of her own. In my opinion, she was best at loving people. I still can't believe she's gone.

I am so grateful that the Lord allowed us that one last visit. I hope I hid my surprise at how much she'd aged; at the time I didn't know the details of how sick she was. I guess you don't tell people everything.

After our meal we prayed together, holding hands. They were seeking God's wisdom because they had to make a choice between two different approaches to her heart problem, which involved a bad valve. I prayed for unity of mind for them, that all the family would be in agreement as to what was the best approach.

A few days later I called to see how their consultation had gone.

"Oh, we really appreciated your prayers, Dear! The Lord answered them; we all think the one method is the best way to go. You were such a blessing to us; I have a lot of peace, especially seeing how the Lord delivered you this past weekend...." Always back to me. Always encouraging others. That was Ann.

Tuesday, I called to tell her how much I loved her and that I would be praying.

Wednesday morning was her surgery, and that afternoon she was out and stable.

Thursday morning, I texted Boyd and he replied she was in the presence of the Lord.

The blood dropped to my feet and I immediately called. Boyd explained that she'd had a lot of pain, the valve failed, her heart stopped, and the doctors couldn't start it again.

Now this is what I want to tell you. The night before her death, during our church's Bible study, I had become very sad. I didn't know why. I left as soon as we were finished because I was crying. I drove home with a heaviness in my chest and many tears. I thought of Ann because of the type of my physical discomfort, but I wasn't really worried. I'd been told she was recovering and stable.

I don't want to open a New-Age can of worms here. Every New-Age can is full of worms anyway, as any Christian knows.

I know I could have been experiencing some undefined anxiety, some latent emotional backlash, even indigestion. But I just can't help but wonder if that sadness and heaviness was related to my dear friend's dying. Has anything like that ever happened to you?

I know of people who've sat bolt upright in bed out of a sound sleep because something has happened to a loved one. I also have friends who carry on running conversations with their dogs. (I might be one of those people.) We don't take the dog conversations seriously. But I don't know if there's a Biblical explanation for the midnight wakings. Do you?

Paul says in II Corinthians 11:29, *Who is weak, and I am not weak? Who is offended, and I burn not?* This at least describes a very close connection with other believers. We know the Lord takes the persecutions of His own so personally, as if done to Him, and the kindnesses, too. He lives inside us; we are one with Him and with each other. There might be some coincident mysteries that intrude upon this earthly pale.

But here is a happy thought: Ann is not only with the Lord, she's with her dear brother who went before her, a godly man whom she has missed terribly. Not to mention countless other members of her family that I've not yet had the pleasure to meet.

At Bible study, despite my mysterious feelings, I had thanked God for bringing Ann through her surgery. And then she died. When a friend reminded me that "It was her time," I felt immediately comforted. For the Christian that is no cliché. *In whose hand is the soul of every living thing, and the breath of all mankind* (Job 12:10). For the child of God, it is a wonderful reminder that nothing went wrong. There were no mishaps, no mistakes to blame on a doctor or computer. My dear Ann had simply lived the last earthly day of her life, as ordained by her Heavenly Father.

Certainly, God loses nothing. Our salvation is completely sure because we are love gifts from the Father to the Son. On Christ's account, and for His sake alone, none of His own will be lost, but we will all rise together on that Great Last Day. I miss my dear Ann so much. But not for long, and not for always. We will hold hands again, and sing, and rejoice in the presence of the Lord. That is our Father's will, and it will surely come to pass.

I guess I should mention that even the camper broke on the way home. My neighbors helped me push it into the garage: "Does it look crooked to you?"

Never mind. Strained axles and a crooked camper were not enough to keep Chloe and me from Ann's memorial. We made the trip together, to honor my friend who honored God and others with her life.

There are no tears where you are, dearest Ann, and one day mine will also be forgotten. Thank you for being such a loving friend to me.

And this is the Father's will which hath sent me, that of all which he hath given me I should lose nothing, but should raise it up again at the last day. And this is the will of him that sent me, that every one which seeth the Son, and believeth on him, may have everlasting life: and I will raise him up at the last day.
John 6:39-40

24

Rewriting History

*Blessed is the man that walketh not in the counsel of the ungodly,
nor standeth in the way of sinners,
nor sitteth in the seat of the scornful.*
Psalms 1:1

I was sitting on a too-small and too-hard stool in Julia's unfinished kitchen, facing a book titled *Cooking with Cannabis*. "A housewarming gift," she told me. You would think a hairdresser's friends might have given her a mirror, since her impromptu salon was not so equipped.

My dear friend Rodney, who has embraced an "alternate lifestyle," is familiar with Julia's scissoring skills. He kindly gave me a haircut with her for Christmas, on the side, on the stool, in the kitchen.

I liked Julia. She did a good job on my hair, although she cut it way too short (I had no way of monitoring.) We had a pleasant back and forth. She'd left a message on my home phone, so I guessed aloud that she must have discovered I'm a Christian. (Chloe barks *Amen!* after a reference to Christ's authority before the beep sounds.) The topic turned to God.

Julia had tried some denominations, preferring Catholicism, although she wasn't practicing.

"Have you met the God of the Bible?" I offered.

"Yes...in the Old Testament He was very harsh."

She continued, "I mean, why would a God of love care who we love?" I sensed a small bomb being dropped along with too much hair. What could I say that wouldn't potentially get back to Rodney and possibly damage a relationship I've prayed and worked very hard to nurture? I sat dumbly, vulnerable under her scissors, my back and other areas hurting.

I am not hiding the truth from my friend Rodney. He knows right from wrong. And I'm pretty sure he's read the Bible. But neither am I declaring the full truth to him, at least not yet. He hasn't backed me into a conversational corner where I would have to speak up or compromise God's honor. I continue to pray about that moment. Meanwhile, I believe he's ashamed, and unable to believe he is loved for more reasons than his lifestyle. Shame can certainly lead us to repentance; shame can be good. It can also kill you. I desperately want him to know how much he is cared for. I desperately want Rodney to have Life.

But what bothered me most about my styling session with Julia was not the stool, the book, or the scalping. It was my internal response to the seductive sound of Julia's voice. She was standing behind me, speaking softly in my ear with words that begged to sink down into my heart, take root, and sprout into forbearing flora that would bow sweetly to any passing breeze, casting seeds that made perfect sense to the world. Why indeed would a loving God care?

The New Tolerance is everywhere. It's successful, it's in-your-face, and it's not just tolerant, it's the right-thing-to-do. It's beyond live-and-let-live. It's now a must-have. It's talk shows, glamor, and money. It's "heroes" who are brave enough to be who they aren't, or change who they are with one-hundred percent insurance coverage signed into law. In fact, it's law itself. It's today, of course, but we can make it yesterday, too.

And if I'm not careful, sometimes I'm afraid I'll believe it.

Television is a powerful brain-altering weapon. I try to focus on older shows, written while some giants were still sleeping and before the Sexual Agenda came out armed and fighting. One of my recent discoveries was a new-ish show that takes place in the fifties. Four women who were code-crackers during World War Two reunite—they're smart, loyal, and surrounded by turquoise appliances, atomic laminate, and starburst mirrors. (They have mirrors.)

I was all settled in one evening, relaxed and unsuspecting, when in waltzed the twenty-first century to take over my show. Seventy years just up and disappeared during an episode starring the nobly oppressed, unjustly accused, and (supposedly) growing homosexual majority of humanity. A thrilling chase scene, all chrome and fins, culminated in a full, flat-on-the-mouth kiss between two of the heroes, both men. I didn't get my hand up over my eyes in time. The women were in allegiance with themselves as well—the smart women who didn't need men, just like the noble men who didn't need women. *Even their women did change the natural use into that which is against nature* (Romans 1:26). One touching scene had my two (formerly) favorite characters summing up the "truth:"

"We are who we are. We love who we love."

I think they know my hairdresser.

See how even the past has been rewritten? See how the "new ideals" can be retrofitted to become the old familiar ways, tucked in amongst the bobby socks and colorful appliances? See how easily I can be tempted to forget my Maker, to whom I should have respect? It all looks so plausible on the screen; it sounds so sensible when whispered in the ear. Or shouted from the rooftops.

That's what I resent. Not people themselves, caught in sin—because I, too, have been responsible for so much damage in my life. I balk at the normalization, the glorification, the promotion and exaltation of sin. I'm angry that it's everywhere I turn, subtle and not. Aren't you? It's where we least expect it: popping up on YouTube, at the elementary school, flashing by in ads where men wear lipstick, where children disguise their genders in rainbow swimsuits. It grieves me. It grieves our Holy God. And it doesn't help anyone.

It's a fine line to walk, loving people like my friend Rodney while hating his sin. Loving people while being aware of an unholy agenda, protecting our own hearts from influence and keeping them with all diligence: this is the calling of those who love God. Getting close without getting tainted is a challenge requiring supernatural grace and direction. The historical script-tampering we need is not the kind that twists our sins into virtues, but that which wrenches them away from us, fully and finally, by the life, death and resurrection of the Son of God. He alone can satisfy the longing soul and subdue the madness overtaking us.

> The King of Love my Savior is...
> by His stripes we are healed.

25

Carsick

I love cars. I guess I inherited that from my father.

When we were growing up, he raced them. Our quiet suburban streets became his Autobahn as he swung the family station wagon into the curves at high speed. From the back seat, I imagined him trying to make the doors fly open so all of us would fall out and he could go on alone. Early Saturday mornings would find him with his head under the hood of his Austin Healey, loudly revving the engine while my mother fielded calls from the neighbors.

All of my father's sports cars were convertibles. My favorite was his pale-yellow Triumph TR3. One day, in a surprising display of fatherly attentiveness, he took me for a spin. In spite of the dreadful babushka my mother made me wear, I was thrilled—thrilled merely to be taken for a ride by my just-out-of-reach father, but in a TR3, no less, with the top down.

In my early twenties, I learned to drive my used Honda Civic stick-shift on its maiden voyage home from the Auto Mall, accompanied by two young males who shouted instructions as we went. Hills and all. That was when I started to enjoy driving.

I'm not terribly skilled, nor aggressive, but when I bought a brand-new turbo Volkswagen Golf, I discovered the exhilaration of being able to not only get ahead, but also to get away. Sadly, this served to fuel my growing impatience behind the wheel. If this kind of thing is genetic, I might again cite my father. I recall the story of him being caught behind a slow driver. When she didn't move fast enough, he simply pushed her through the intersection. I might not be that bad.

During a warranty period, one must go to the dealership for everything—including oil changes. (I'm a "wait" person, not a "drop-off.") All those hours of waiting during maintenance on my VW brought me into a kind of relationship with the service manager, henceforth referred to as "New-Age Steve."

As background, you should understand that my cars have always had Christian signage. Hanging from my rear-view mirror in this one was a little wooden plaque given by a friend, a helpful reminder to myself: *I Work for God*. On my first dealership appointment it caught the eye of New-Age Steve. "I work for God, too!" he announced.

That opened the door for five years of Dealership Discussions during which we discovered how completely opposed our views of God really were. I talked sin, atonement, and bodily resurrection, while Steve talked Deepak Chopra and Dr. Oz, neither of whom agree with traditional Christianity. Sure, Steve explained, he used to think "that way." He used to go to church. He used to be married. Then he became enlightened.

The divorce destroyed his ability to trust. With his piercing blue eyes filling up, right there behind the service desk one day (where was everyone?), Steve poured out the story of how happy he had been with his wife. He was married for life and thought everything was fine. Then he came home one day, and she told him it was over.

He nearly killed himself, his depression was so great. He bought a gun. But he was helped by a friend who was aware enough to step in. Thank God, we could say.

As he spoke, I wondered if getting over marriage was connected to Steve's getting over God. Turned out, he discovered he was very happy alone, and his New Age god made no demands on him.

Steve told me he found out he didn't need anyone at all, that he'd been wrong all along about relationships.

Five years and many oil changes later, on the very day the warranty expired, my little car flashed her check-engine light, shook like a leaf, and fell apart before my eyes. But not without costing me a lot of money. After one month of repairs and two outrageous invoices, I picked her up from the dealership. And the next morning, she still shook like a leaf. I figured Steve wasn't the only one who'd been wrong about relationships. Maybe I had been naïve in thinking Steve was my friend.

As with the finger of God on my bumper, I was pushed into the arms of the competition. I rushed to trade in my dying Volkswagen before the check-engine light could come back on and she stopped running altogether. My neighbors advised me to write a letter of complaint to the American Headquarters and attach a picture of the new-used Kia Soul the Lord provided to get me out of my terrible jam.

Instead, I wrote a personal letter to New-Age Steve. It occurred to me that the Stateside Division might not care one tiny bit about what happened. Perhaps Steve himself wouldn't care, either, since he might have known that they hadn't really fixed my car. But just in case Steve was uninformed, in paragraph one I mentioned the king's ransom I'd thrown out the window in his direction. First things first. Then I reminded him of his relationship with God.

During our time together, I had given him a copy of my first Christian CD (which he said he'd never opened), some of my Christian prose (which he said he'd never read), and an mp3 home recording of a new song. During an oil change I had cornered him into playing the mp3 while I stood there staring at him. He told me the tone of my song was somber, and suggested, "Why don't you write about Him?"*

That really struck me. After all of Steve's protesting against the God of the Bible, something still told him that, even though He wasn't mentioned, Christ was the answer to the sadness in my song. I knew that, of course. But part of Steve knew it, too. Not the newly enlightened Steve, the one who didn't need anyone anymore. But the former Steve, the one I had addressed in my letter.

"You are of more value than many cars," I wrote. I gave him the reference, Matthew 10:31, thinking he might still have his Bible on a dusty shelf somewhere in that empty house.

I continued: "We are, in God's own Words, 'A people I have formed for Myself'" (Isaiah 43:21). I explained to Steve that real relationship is the heart behind redemption. That the Son of God took on human nature, not that of bulls, goats, angels, or machines, but of people. He became a man to rescue his own possession. He married us, body and soul.

One divorce is too much for anyone. I prayed that Steve would return to the God who is faithful and true—who would never come home one day and tell him it's over.

This faithful God prevented my writing that complaint to the Head Office. Had I written it, the only thing that I would have accomplished would have been the wiping out of five years of witnessing to Steve. In potentially hurting him, I'd have handed him (along with my charge card) another excuse to disbelieve in the God Who Cares, to deny Him again and bury his head in his "I am enough" philosophy.

What is left after the ruin of marriages, metal, and zoom? The souls of men, the lives of people, the things God (the Christian one) cares about.

Now then, my new-used Kia has many good qualities, the best one being that it starts up when I turn the key. I am grateful, I really am. I think, however, the Lord has a mind to sanctify and humble me as I drive. I must need it badly. This is a very slow car. It has just a few ponies, a tiny bit of torque, and very little zoom. Instead of sighing about the people in front of me, I am sighing for myself. I will not be pushing anyone through any intersection; you might be inclined to give me a nudge. If you are behind me, please bear with me. I am pedaling as fast as I can.

Fear ye not therefore, ye are of more value than many sparrows.
Matthew 10:31

*Here is the sad song I shared with Steve, replete with longing for the former days and the childhood that was never mine.

Black and White

I am going out of style, I guess I knew that.
I keep reaching back for something that's not there.
All my made-up friends and families are gone now.
They come streaming in...from a satellite somewhere.

I miss those snapshots, The way they smelled,
The way they curled up at the edges
If you didn't paste them tight
Into those big books that hold my youth;
When the world was black and white.

Do you see that little girl? I know she's frightened.
She's still looking for the world she wanted then.
She can't pull it up on YouTube or on Facebook.
Blow the dust away...still can't try it all again.

I miss those snapshots...

Girls were pink, boys were blue,
You know we always had a little wiggle-room.
But we were safe, because that net
Kept us from leaping into something we'd regret.

Please don't shrug those shoulders,
Not that vacant stare.
It's not just that I'm older,
There's a way to care,
And you can learn it, too.
I have confidence in you.

I miss those snapshots,
The way they smelled,
The way they curled up at the edges
If you didn't paste them tight
Into those big books that hold my youth;
When the world
Was black and white.
–Susan Piper, "Black and White"

26

Dry Your Eyes

If there's one shred-of-a-good thing to be said about being out of work for a year during a global pandemic, it is this: it gave my little Chloe the time she needed to die.

I had begun steeling myself for her death about four years earlier, around her tenth birthday. This is what I always do, isn't it. I start preparing myself for sadness way ahead of time, thinking that when the tragedy finally strikes, somehow I'll be ready. But of course it doesn't work. All that preparedness just kind of takes over the life I am living in the meantime.

Chloe was mildly ill during the spring of that awful year, when all our nursing homes closed their doors. She had a cough that my vet continually brushed off, chalking it up to allergies. He called it "tracheitis" and repeatedly threw prednisone at us, letting it go at that.

He was wrong, but looking back, I now see that as a gift. It was easier for me not to know how ill she was. There was nothing that could have been done to save her.

Certainly she was slowing down, but I thought that was to be expected because she was approaching fourteen years old. Then she stopped eating, and we returned to the vet. He told me to leave her so that they could run some tests. Finally.

Some eternal hours later, the doctor called. "Chloe's kidneys are functioning at twenty-five percent. She has a tumor in her chest and spots on her liver." Raging against the message and the messenger, I raced to the office to rescue my little girl—as if I really could. "I didn't think Chloe was going home," the receptionist said. "Oh yes she is, and right away," I muttered under my breath.

With some meds and special food, she ate a bit for a day. Then, at midnight on the fourth of July, which is when we do things like this, I took her to the twenty-four-hour emergency vet for a second opinion. Nine hundred dollars later, they confirmed her diagnosis.

The emotionless on-call vet gave me two options: put Chloe down now or take her home for some kind of hospice-long-goodbye. Option number one was out of the question. No unsympathetic vet would be ending my dog's life. The girl who wrote up the bill said, "Oh, I've never seen one of these," remarking at the uniqueness of my little girl's breed. She had no idea how special she really was.

In the end, we shared five final days of "hospice." I followed Chloe around with peanut butter on my finger and a little bowl of water, but she wouldn't touch a thing. I prayed over her, asking the Lord to take her, but He wouldn't do a thing. I sang hymns to her while she slept, found a shovel, and started digging a hole in the yard.

Do you know how much strength it takes to dig a large hole? Much more than I had. My neighbor stood at the back fence. "Did you lose your little dog?" she asked. "Not yet," was all I could stammer. My other neighbor and his father came to help me carve out a resting place deep and wide enough so that Chloe's sweet little body would be safe from other animals and could sleep quietly under the ground.

The internet says that after five days of not eating, a dog is truly suffering. Suffering was my line in the sand—and we had now crossed over it. I bundled Chloe up in her little bed on the front seat and we went back to the emergency practice. (I didn't think I could hold myself together in front of the people who knew us at our own vet.) It was Tuesday morning, regular office hours now. I was praying for a kind doctor this time.

On our first car ride home together all those years ago, she'd thrown up in the back seat, and this continued for quite some time during our bumpy adjustment period. But as I learned patience and she learned routine, she had grown to enjoy all our traveling. On our last trip she sat with her head up, watching the world go by.

This doctor was very kind and gentle indeed. My hand was under Chloe's head as she fell asleep. I laid her back in her burial bed and carried her out to the car through the side door, the one you exit when you have a little body like this with you. People coming in stepped back involuntarily; even if they couldn't see clearly, they knew.

I buried her all by myself. Throwing dirt back in is nearly as difficult as digging it out, and in the middle of July, it was all a miserable business. But I didn't want anyone to help me. I worked and worked, with all the tears streaming down my face.

Chloe brought joy to hundreds, probably thousands of people. I can't count them; I don't even remember them all. I was given a jewel. That's how I saw her—as a beautiful, irreplaceable jewel. A breed above my standing, that someone like me could never afford, a dog that "no one gives away" had been given to me. And now, without her, I didn't know what I would do.

The last enemy to be destroyed is death.
   I Corinthians 1:26

27

The Conditions of Love

I was new in Christ, and new to my nursing home ministry, when a new patient arrived.

Ray was huge. More than morbidly obese, his tattoos had expanded with him. Lying in a specially-sized bed, missing a leg, his shaved head and earring glowed. "Take as much time with him as you want," I was instructed.

Since I did not yet have a canine partner to put forth as an ice breaker (or shield), I hid my unremarkable self behind my feeble little nylon-string guitar. I approached Ray with fear and trembling, armed not with Led Zeppelin, but with old-fashioned hymns and a fledgling witness for the Lord.

Amazingly, we became friends. I learned as much about Ray's life as he would tell me: his Harley and his biker gang, his father's religious background. I dredged up a James Taylor song to try to please him. He asked questions and the Holy Spirit gave me answers. We ended our visits with prayer.

Ray was matter of fact when he prayed. "Jesus, we need some help here..." and he would present his list. He had no learned religiosity to restrict any of his thoughts. He was simple and straight to the point. He touched my heart.

Ray shared my excitement as I finished my first Christian CD, so I mailed him a copy. Somehow he got my phone number and left a high-velocity, continuous-play message of congratulations on my machine. The next time I visited him I was greeted with a more personalized view of his sentiments. Walking into Ray's room I met myself, blown up to poster size and taped to his closet door. (Someone had enlarged the CD insert picture of me.) He'd made me the rock star of the nursing home. It was a little embarrassing.

I was given great freedom at this home and worked for three hours at a stretch, wandering from floor to floor—health care, memory care, and rehabilitation. The facility was joined to a hospital, so when Ray's kidneys were finally shutting down, I was allowed to go through and visit him. He was preparing for his death and had already asked me, "Will you come?"

The intensive care nurses gave me access because I had my Bible with me and someone mistook me for a pastor. I read to Ray about the necessity of faith in Christ alone, the promise of our resurrection, our hope of a glorious future. "Do you believe this?" Ray nodded his assent from behind the big oxygen mask covering his face. All I could see were his eyes.

When it came time for his funeral, I really wondered what kind of coffin they could find for Ray. There was an incident where the staff couldn't get him on the elevator. But when I first entered the church and saw his casket from a distance, Ray's once-swollen body looked so small. Maybe it was the fluid and sickness that had left him, but to me it was a testimony to the reality of his soul, which had fled the corruption of this mortal coil. I had hope that he was safe with the Lord.

I started walking forward to pay my respects, but on my way up the aisle I was stopped cold by a familiar face looking out of his coffin, propped up on the inside edge of the lid. It was me. The CD insert, the actual one, was tucked in with Ray's body. I quickly dissolved into the nearest pew and snuck out as soon as the service was over.

Once in the car, I couldn't stop crying. But my tears were selfish, and not for the loss of Ray. I cried because he loved me. He loved me far more than I had ever loved him. I would never have even conceived of putting his picture into my coffin. That kind of love was devastating to me.

When I was growing up, love came with all the sticky trappings of a giant spider's web: powerful, abhorrent, confusing. It's not that I don't feel love, oh, I do, and very deeply. But I have so much trouble trying to connect it to another human being without complication.

I carry a deep loneliness. It's as if the bottom half of my life has come loose and I've been treading water, searching for it for years. Some kind of undergirding substance seems to be missing from me.

But when Ray looked at me, he saw nothing lacking. Any reserve I felt in my heart didn't stop him from wanting me with him forever. He attached no conditions to his love.

This is the kind of devastating and unconditional love that God offers to the world. But unless we are united to Christ, we can't claim it. We'll always be hiding in the pew or crying in the car and that love will remain beyond our understanding and out of our reach.

Look with me at John 3:16: *For God so loved the world that He gave His only begotten Son, that whosoever believeth in him should not perish, but have everlasting life.*

This famous verse doesn't just tell us that God loves humanity "so" much. It also tells us *how* He loves. The New Living Translation seems to say it best: *For this is how God loved the world....*

A holy God loved sinners in this way: *that He gave His one and only son.*

The love of God organically lives and breathes in Christ Jesus our Lord. Where else will we find the forgiveness we need, the holiness we lack, the fullness of Him who fills our emptiness in every way?

The truth is, because of sin, we are separated from God by mountains of conditions we can never overcome. But His heart is so generous that by giving us His Son, God answered His own holy demands. Every requirement was met by the sinless, obedient life of our Savior. When God joins us to Jesus by faith—*in this way*—He can shower us with His unconditional love. And in Christ, we can finally receive it.

Blessedly, it's never been about you, or me, or Ray. It's always been, and always will be about Jesus—and the infinite love the Father has for His Son.

To the praise of the glory of his grace,
wherein he hath made us accepted in the beloved.
Ephesians 3:6

28

Heaven

People have made millions writing books about their visits to heaven. Some have confessed to lying about those visits and presumably repented.

I took my own trip to heaven while imprisoned on the isle of unemployment during the tribulation of our world-wide plague. I didn't make millions, but then, I was only gone for the day. I traveled as a passenger with my new friend Paul, who was training me to make deliveries for Meals on Wheels.

Truth be told, my primary assignment with the meal delivery ministry was in the purgatory of kitchen duty. Home delivery was my heart's desire, but they could only promise occasional opportunities for substitute driving. I clutched at that wilted straw while I took my place behind the steam tables. But I soon learned I was not built for the endless standing and bending and reaching that the job of filling food trays, washing down stainless-steel table legs, and loading huge double-door refrigerators required. Blessedly, after two days in the sweatshop of "purification," my soul was sprung to the high road that led to glory. Meal delivery training day had dawned.

Please understand, as we head to my guided tour of heaven, it might not be what you've imagined. I will tell you that the throne room is located just beyond Helen's front door, where Paul and I make our first delivery of the morning.

Helen is legally blind and welcomes us from her wheelchair parked beside a yellowing Formica countertop. Surrounding her are six dead mice still in their traps, soon to be interred by Paul via open burial in the kitchen can. A white plastic knife balances on the edge of a lid, aimed at the peanut butter, ready for Paul to reload the arsenal for the next slaughter of vermin.

Circling our feet is Helen's canine companion, a brown, bug-eyed Peter Lorre on four skinny legs. When my vinyl-clad fingers scratch his back, he springs up, panting furiously as his nails chip away at the dirty floor.

"That's what Baby likes, that's what he's looking for!" Helen responds, defending Baby's clattering joy.

The marriage supper is surprisingly meager, but at least it's cooked and nutritionally balanced. Paul describes it to Helen. "Turkey breast (one slice), seasoned potatoes (three slices), and cauliflower. Mandarin oranges, I think this is pineapple, two milks, and three breads. Oh, and a cookie!" (Comments, mine.)

"I have your mail, Helen," I report, "but it's from a lawn company and it's addressed to Current Resident, so I think it's junk. I'll throw it away?" I touch her shoulder with my gloved hand; she reaches up for it immediately, though we've just met.

It's dark in the throne room as well. "Helen, is there anything I can do for you while we're here?" I ask.

"Oh yes, dear, would you change that bulb at the bottom of the basement stairs?"

Throwing my shimmering cape over my shoulder to avoid tripping, I fly down the steps into action. How many Super-Christian women does it take to change a lightbulb? At the touch of my skillful fingers the bulb is broken in the socket and dangles there like an ancient tooth.

"You'd better turn it off," Helen says. I pull the chain and we are safe.

Paul, with his years of experience, is the man. He keeps a tool kit in the truck. I am privileged to hold the flashlight as he removes the damaged bulb and replaces it with another (unbeknownst to us) bad bulb. He pulls on the chain which no longer moves, thanks to my expert assistance. "I didn't know it had a chain!" Helen calls from the top of the stairs.

Twenty minutes later, with the power still on, as I helpfully continue to hold the flashlight, Paul disconnects the receptacle, removes the chain, replaces the bulb again, and there is light. He is the man, as I have said.

When we started my training day that morning, Paul had informed me of the ninety deliveries we would make. In one day. "Oh, you can't stop," he said. Helen was our exception.

I had had such high hopes for that job. I thought it would return me to "My Peeps." I saw myself knocking on door after door (but not ninety of them) smiling, waving, delivering life-saving manna and cheering someone's day, especially my own. But there is not a GPS known to man that would take me to ninety destinations in one day. I can get lost in a parking lot. I would again forget to close the truck's refrigerated unit door ("You left that door wide open!" Paul said.) The food would go bad. The police would have to follow the trail of little potato slices to rescue me, escorting me back to the main roads, calling ahead to Non-Profit Headquarters and reporting: "We've found her, but the meals, well, how many are there supposed to be?"

I had to quit, but I hated to be "a quitter." I had wanted to be a Christian example, going the extra two miles (via GPS) and shining for Jesus. But my little lampstand, once filled with the hope of driving and delivering, had been completely drained in just one exhausting day. And I couldn't face those steam tables again.

Who builds a tower without sitting down first to count the cost, to see if she has enough to finish it? (Luke 14:28-30). I didn't know it would be so tall, and I so small, and so embarrassed.

It was best I realized my own limitations and resign before something worse happened to me.

But God was so kind. Red-faced or not, along with the other Paul (II Corinthians 12:2-4), I was given the glorious reprieve of a near-life experience. Transported from the aching emptiness of my own private island, I had been sent by the Spirit into the heart-pumping, soul-freeing, self-forgetting service of Someone Else. I went to heaven, however clumsily, and came back, permitted to tell the tale.

I filed Helen's memory away, with so many others, as I waited for the day when the long veil of the virus would be torn in two. The day when the gates of the nursing homes would lift up their heads to welcome me and my guitar into Paradise once again.

And the city had no need of the sun,
neither of the moon,
to shine in it:
for the glory of God did lighten it,
and the Lamb is the light thereof.
Revelation 21:23

29
Memorials

Walk into my home, and you won't see any pictures of my deceased parents. None. Not even the historic snapshots my kind cousin sent me because he assumed I would want to frame and hang them.

I have one photo of my father (with his new wife torn out). It is hiding in a drawer in the living room because I can't look at him without crying. I saved a voicemail from him on my answering machine, but I don't listen to that, either. My mother, in all her beauty, is nowhere to be found; even writing about these things brings tears. How could I possibly have a peaceful home if their pictures were emotionally assaulting me from my very own walls? I wouldn't be able to sleep at night. I have enough trouble as it is.

In an unguarded moment, I once shared these secret thoughts with a sister in the Lord. She shook her finger at me and accused, "You have not forgiven your mother!" I think she's wrong, but I didn't shake back. I think I have forgiven, mostly. But the pain is still there. I don't dwell on it, unless another pain comes along and wakes everything up. There was no reconciliation before my mother's death. That doesn't mean I haven't forgiven her. It just means she still breaks my heart. So, where is the profit in looking at her picture on my wall every day?

My dear father took his own life, so how in the world could I walk past him on my way to the kitchen every morning without being reminded? Isn't that what pictures are for? Little memorials to keep our loved ones close when they have gone away? Maybe if I lived in a mansion, I could hang all those pictures in a back room at the end of the east wing somewhere and just keep the door locked. I'd allow my servants to go in and dust them, but don't ask any questions. Not if you want to work for me, folks.

My home *is* crowded, however, with pictures of Chloe. She was the most photogenic one in our family of two, my family consisting of me and my dog. I used to joke and say she was adopted, and that's why you couldn't see a family resemblance. I wanted to be as pretty as she. I am still having a very hard time with her loss.

But hard time or not, I never, ever, want to remove a single one of her pictures. And at this point I am so determined to keep them on display that I won't even move one to a different shelf. All pictures—and her beds, her little sweaters (this is getting maudlin) must remain exactly where they are. Chloe's pictures don't attack me; they bring me comfort, sad as they make me feel. They are precious little memorials. They make me cry, but I won't even let the servants dust them. I take care of them personally.

I am sure, I would bet my life in fact, that most people do not understand the level of attachment I had to Chloe; and if they do understand, they think it's unnatural. Or *unhealthy*—a code word some folks use when they are looking down their noses at you but want to appear concerned, in my opinion.

There are a few blessed exceptions, thank you, the Lord Himself being one: *But the poor man had nothing, save one little ewe lamb, which he had bought and nourished up: and it grew up together with him, and with his children; it did eat of his own meat, and drank of his own cup, and lay in his bosom, and was unto him as a daughter* (II Samuel 12:3).

You might remember that parable. Nathan the prophet shamed David the king with those words after he stole Bathsheba away from her husband. And as we know, the Lord isn't really speaking of a man's lamb; he's speaking of his wife. But why would God write that way if He didn't appreciate our love for our pets? I hear the Lord's deep understanding in this verse, and I'm not the only one.

Soon after my Chloe died, I was explaining her passing to a small group of people after Sunday service. Of course I was crying. Standing beside me was a single woman who lives with five cats. We started to exchange end-of-life stories, the pet kind, I mean, and the trauma that accompanies these things. I started to say, "God knows how we feel, remember that story of Nathan and—"

"The little lamb!" she interrupted, her head bobbing expansively. People might look down their noses at her too, but the Lord never does.

I have memorialized and honored my little late companion and ministry partner in a number of ways that bring me some satisfaction. Her eighteen sympathy cards are displayed on the dining room table with a tiny vase of flowers from my hydrangea bushes. (I know the cards are addressed to me, but they're in honor of Chloe, so I prefer to say *she* received them. I imagine that's part of my previously cited unhealthiness.) Her grave is the prettiest part of the back yard, on the inside corner of the low back fence. It is decorated with yellow evening primroses, a painted green and purple stone, a heart-shaped rock, five big landscaping stones, yellow and pink windmill flowers from the Dollar Store, a mum in a pink pot, fresh potting soil, and a chunk of a tree inscribed with "Jesus Never Fails." I don't know if burying a pet is legal in my state, but I'm sure I have a sufficient amount of camouflage so as not to attract attention.

I bumped into an acquaintance who had known us as a pair. Bypassing the standard inquiry into my health, her first question was, "Where's your little dog?" When I explained, she looked away, saying, "They're just like children...I lost my baby boy last January. It was cancer." Hers was the big loss and mine was no comparison, except to my own heart. But she stooped down and acknowledged my sorrow with me. She was so kind.

"Misery loves company" is usually a sarcastic expression, but grief truly does love company. Grief needs company. Grief backs up and calms down and lies quietly at the feet of a fellow sufferer.

My bosom friend Lena could educate the overly "concerned." She lives alone and lost her own little best friend some years ago. She still has the brush that holds a bit of left-over fur. Lena walked through the last year of Chloe's life with me, asking every day on the phone, "How's our baby?" Whenever we would visit, she would feed Chloe from her wheelchair while Chloe did nothing but chew and look adorable.

Lena's home is also adorned with many pictures of my little-miss-photogenic. I made one last montage for her and delivered it on my bicycle, wrapped in foam and tucked into the basket.

I had decorated two matching Dollar Store frames with cut-outs from greeting cards and Elmer's glue, one for each of us, which gave me a flashback of picking dandelions for my mother at seven years old. (I told myself this was different). It was the last photo of Chloe and me, taken exactly seventeen days before she died. I am holding her next to my face, my hands under her paws. On Lena's frame, I put the word *Wonderful*. When she first met Chloe, she'd taken her little head in her hands and exclaimed, "Oh, you're the most wonderful dog in the world!" When she opened the picture, we both sat there and cried.

They say that people who have been happily married have the best chance of a second happy marriage after the death of a spouse. With two failed marriages and no children, I do not have the affinity with intimacy that I would prefer, but I know that I have one proven track record that bears repeating. I can love a dog. I can do that so well, in fact, that even now, folks are preparing to bend their heads and look down their noses at me in great concern. Because somehow, somewhere, God must have another friend for me.

O LORD, thou knowest:
remember me...
Jeremiah 15:15

30

John Prine

At sixteen years old, with my new driver's license propelling me as a bullet to stardom, I aimed myself toward Cleveland's bars to sing and play my Martin guitar (just like John Prine's). How this was legal, I don't know.

"Paradise," "Sam Stone," "Illegal Smile," these were some of the celebrated creations of the hero of my heathen hippie-youth. I had memorized Prine's first self-titled album and incorporated his songs fully into my sets, causing my agent to question my show-business savvy: "What's with all the John Prine?"

This wonderful singer-songwriter was, sadly, my first personal connection to death when the pandemic hit. John was 73 when he died on April 7, 2020. He'd come through some bouts with cancer; I'm sure that contributed to the aging-artist persona captured on the cover of *The Tree of Forgiveness*, his final album.

When I learned of his death, I immediately searched the internet for evidence of Christ in Prine's writings or interviews. I hoped there might be something I didn't know. That title, *The Tree of Forgiveness*, encouraged me. Who is that Tree of Forgiveness but the Lord Jesus?

But instead of signs of real redemption, I discovered songs of smoking and drinking vodka in heaven. I learned that Prine's latest wife had "washed away his sins." Using the words "fifty-fifty shot" in a late interview, John explained, "There's life and then there's death."[1] Or, to quote the hopeless situation in his song "Sam Stone": "Jesus Christ died for nothing, I suppose."[2] To me, this was more than artistic expression. This was the testimony of my icon.

God gave John the gifts of insight and wordcraft, though he acknowledged Him not. "Hello in There" is a perfect example, the main prompt for my sentimental searching. Written when John was in his early twenties, it is understated, tender brilliance:

> ...Ya' know that old trees just grow stronger,
> And old rivers grow wilder ev'ry day,
> Old people just grow lonesome
> Waiting for someone to say, "Hello in there, hello."
>
> So if you're walking down the street sometime
> And spot some hollow ancient eyes,
> Please don't just pass 'em by and stare
> As if you didn't care, say, "Hello in there, hello."
> –John Prine, "Hello in There"

That song means even more to me now because of my nursing home experiences. Not that I could visit my captive friends in the time of the virus. Because, aside from the devastation, we all suffered the unnatural sorrow of human separation. Six feet apart, no touching, only eyes above a mask. "So Far Away," says Carole King.

---

1. https://pitchfork.com/features/overtones/life-death-and-john-prine/

2. *Sam Stone*, John Prine

What is it about people's faces? When I think of how inexplicably wonderfully we are made, I see the crowning touch of our reflection of God in our expressions, in how much we say without a word. I love to watch signing for the deaf in church. There, the spoken Word of God is simultaneously animated by face and fingers in silent drama—broadly, brightly, with joy and hand-drawn tears. Our glorious faces, wherein few of us can hide our hearts, were obscured by fear and covered by cloth during the pandemic. The masks were the worst part of all. Yea, if I hadn't been walking through that virus-filled valley, I might not have felt so keenly the loss of Mr. Prine. My emotions were a mess.

I called an optimistic friend before googling John's religion. She generously suggested he might have been a secret Christian, "deep down." An ironic way to excuse a failure to witness, don't you think? Presumably, the deeper one's faith, the more it would bubble up to the surface. I thought about John's platform. If he were a redeemed child of God, how could he have been given such a vehicle and not even mention salvation in Christ? *For whosoever shall be ashamed of me and of my words, of him shall the Son of man be ashamed, when he shall come in his own glory, and in his Father's, and of the holy angels* (Luke 9:26).

No one knows the heart of man except the Lord, and you are free to disagree with me. But sadly, I could uncover no love for Christ in the fruit produced by our talented friend John. That tempered my sentimentality, but also promoted horrific thoughts of eternal punishment. When my father died, hell became much too real to me. My mind was tormented. Finally, out of concern for my senses, I had to decide very purposefully to shut out the thoughts because, simply put, God is always right. I could only rest in that.

My friend and I talked briefly of hell on the phone. We wondered what it would be like if we were in charge of the eternal destinies of men. We decided Purgatory must have been born of such dreams. For us, we would either wave our hands and excuse everybody, or, after having sentenced some to suffering, we would look down mercifully and call out, "You can come out now!" Everyone but Hitler, of course.

Surely if God had not rescued me, I would still be writing meaningless songs of made-up spirituality, lust, and misguided love. But even in my former condition there appeared a song or two that mattered, that spoke of beauty and some kind of truth. God gives many gifts to men; He's kind even to the ungrateful and the wicked.

I would never want to be God, would you? I wouldn't really want to be in charge. But if I were, I would end every disease and bring John Prine back from the dead, and my father, too.

Let's not consider the former things; we have so much to be thankful for now. And I have missed the touch of love so very much. May I never, ever take for granted the hugs and kisses of my friends and the image of God in our beautiful, open, and unveiled faces.

> *My dove in the clefts of the rock,*
> *in the hiding places on the mountainside,*
> *show me your face, let me hear your voice;*
> *for your voice is sweet,*
> *and your face is lovely.*
> Song of Solomon 2:14, NIV

31

Wishy-Washy

I think I am emotionally attached to my washing machine. It's also possible that I use laundry as an excuse to avoid housecleaning. Whenever I feel like a sloth, I just toss in a load. I pretend I'm productive, and at least something gets clean. But it wasn't until my beloved top-loader gave up the ghost that I fully realized my codependence.

One Saturday morning I repeatedly found myself tottering at the brink of the basement stairs, only to recall each time—with a catch in my chest—*No. It's broken.*

And so it was. Sadly, after seven years of a very clean relationship, my washer refused to spin. It seemed headed for the scrap heap. But I needed an experienced professional to determine if it was dead or merely in a coma. Therein was my dilemma. I assumed that a technician would charge me a small fortune just to pad down the basement stairs and run a clicking Geiger-counter tool up and down the control board looking for some sign of life. Then he'd look me in the eye and say it needed a part that would take two weeks to arrive and cost exactly half the price of a new machine. And my dilemma would rise again to the surface, like machine oil on water. Repair or buy new? What was I to do?

A missionary friend in Morocco, whose own washer turns with a wooden hand crank, suggested I ask around. Someone might be upgrading from an older model and would be happy to give it to a sister-in-need. Missionaries are resourceful. In my emulation, I sent an email to the entire church.

Our Pastor Phil was the first to respond. Men like to fix things. He asked many questions, including the model number, and offered to do research to make his own diagnosis. He didn't promise he could make the repair, but he gave me hope. I was grateful to have someone-who-knows-something come alongside me. (I should never have been entrusted with the keys to an entire house. I'm sure I am apartment material, but God was so kind to put me here.)

While I waited for Pastor Phil's diagnosis, I kept praying. The Lord is my husband and my helper; we single women are always storming heaven and YouTube for answers. I told a non-believing friend, "God won't give me a verse in the Bible that tells me whether to repair or replace my washing machine." But I was privately praying He would.

Meanwhile, time was ticking and my clothes were not getting any cleaner (I was forced to clean the house). To check on his progress, I left a teasing voicemail for Pastor Phil: "Is this 'Pastor Phil's Appliance Repair'? I'd like to put in an order...." When I didn't hear back, I decided to google "Washer repair near me." It wouldn't hurt to look.

Up popped "Phil's Appliance Repair." Now that was a quirky coincidence. Or was it the leading of the Lord? I opted for the latter and clicked on the link.

There, I met the company's technicians, Angel, Gabriel, and Marie. Now I was laughing. "Pastor" Phil's Appliance Repair, with Angel, Gabriel and Mary? I went ahead and scheduled.

About an hour later, the real Pastor Phil returned my call. His sources had suggested that my poor machine would need a control board replacement, meaning a brain transplant, not merely an attitude adjustment. It would have been too expensive to fix, so I called the impersonating "Holy Family" repair shop and canceled.

Then our deacons, in response to my churchwide email, came alongside and offered to assist me financially. Moving quickly to take advantage of an online promotion, I drove to the local big-box store to purchase the least expensive washer in their ad. In the car on the way, I prayed to my Lord to hold my hand, go before me, and make sure I was doing the right thing. It was dinnertime, and the store was quiet. I walked to the back and found a woman working next to the appliances.

"Hi, are you in appliances?"

"No, I'm not; I'll get someone for you." Two minutes later she reappeared. "*Chloe* will be right with you…"

Our tender Shepherd has promised to personally lead us along. *He leadeth me beside the still waters* (Psalm 23:2). According to Strong's Concordance, leadeth (Hebrew 5095) means *to run with a sparkle.*

After twenty years, I have a history with my Lord. I know He delights, sings, composes, loves pleasure, creates beauty, and gives us laughter as well as tears. His high and perfect holiness is not dry and brittle. He sparkles! And He wants his children to know who He is.

A famous theologian once said, "If you want to be absolutely sure of God's will, look at what happened yesterday." Simply put, we won't always be certain of God's leading. However, our confidence lies not in our interpretation of His providence, but in the faithfulness of his love. If we know Him, we will eventually know the way.

But let him that glorieth glory in this, that he knoweth and understandeth me, that I am the LORD which exercise lovingkindness, judgment, and righteousness, in the earth: for in these things I delight, saith the LORD.
Jeremiah 9:24

32

Levi

*Do not despise these small beginnings,
for the LORD rejoices to see the work begin...*
Zechariah 4:10, NLT

I don't pay much attention to the news. It's depressing. I remember seeing the images of people in China wearing masks in early 2020 and thinking, "Those poor people." Surely "It," whatever "It" was, would never come here. But part of keeping one's head in the sand is thinking that one would be protected from such things.

I also remember thinking that even though I was self-employed, my safety net was that I kept my eggs in so many different baskets. Five years after relocating to Ohio, I was now working for 21 nursing homes—once, twice, four times per month. If one egg dropped, it wasn't such a big deal. I had all those other baskets to carry me until I could find a replacement.

Flash forward to March of 2020. I remember Monday the 9th, most of all. My phone began ringing constantly that morning, as it never does, and it didn't stop until every nursing home that thought anything of me had called to tell me to stop coming. The rest didn't bother, but I knew. I started writing their names in my journal along with how much income I would be losing...until it didn't matter. It was all gone.

In my fear and isolation, I still had my Chloe to cling to, and cling I did. But there was one bright spot. Miraculously, the president so many people had fussed about made sure that "gig workers" such as I were awarded unemployment. I was still frightened and tearful but not since I'd been an activities director had I ever been paid regularly. Now, more money was electronically arriving than I was used to earning. I might have lost everything. Instead, I painted my kitchen cabinets and paid off my car.

While the world shifted, God let me hold onto Chloe, at least for the first few tremor-filled months. Most of the other loves of my life were locked inside their nursing homes. Those were my people, my friends, both residents and directors. You remember how lonely it was. People stayed home, gained weight, bought puppies.

By July of that year, Choe's dreadful day of death had arrived, and there was no stopping it. I wailed at least as much for her as I had wailed for my father. There is a certain depth of grief that pulls sounds out of you that you never knew you could emit. A few weeks after she died, I remember coming in and throwing down the groceries, shaking the walls in my bitterness of heart. I didn't hold back—I live alone, who would hear me? Opening my eyes, I saw my neighbor pulling weeds on her side of the fence, fifteen feet away. Head down, she was kind enough to just keep digging.

Soon I went online and began looking for a "face," an expression, any reminiscence of my beautiful girl. Never mind observing a proper period of mourning, I couldn't bear the emptiness. I knew I would never replace her, but I was miserable on my own. I tried contacting the breeder who'd given me Chloe. I forwarded her memorial pictures and inquired about another, possibly free friend. She never got back to me.

Then the internet introduced me to the national dog of Cuba, the "Havanese." Small, smart, gentle—we'll discuss that—often used in therapy, and in the circus. That last trait makes sense to me now.

I found a breeder an hour away whose prices were a bit more reasonable than most. In Karen's gallery was a doggie-mom-to-be who looked very much like a smaller version of my Chloe. The puppies were due in August.

I knew I did not want a boy. It had been just us girls here, and I wanted to keep it that way. (I may still have a few "men issues.") I was on the list for girl number three, but she was born a preemie and did not survive, despite my prayers. Telling me the bad news, Karen said, "I still have one beautiful brown boy available." While I hesitated, she added, "Girls will say, 'You should love me.' Boys will say, 'I should love you.'" I thought about it for ten minutes, called her back, and caved.

I had had a girl's name ready, but now I had to re-think. Since he was going to be little, I wanted him to have some respect—nothing like "Sparky" or "Skippy." (He does skip when he runs, it's the cutest thing.) And a Bible name, of course. The Havanese are known as "the Velcro dog" because of their attachment to people. The name Levi, Jacob's third son, means "attached" in Hebrew. Not to mention it's the name of the high-priestly tribe and the dog on *Sue Thomas, F.B.Eye*. Lots of respect there, thank you.

I couldn't go see my puppy during a global plague, so Karen sent videos and pictures. Levi learned his name long before he came home, and I could pick him out of the litter because of one ear that always turned inside out.

On October 10th, I drove out to the country and Karen finally handed me my boy. Pulling his squirming body under my chin, I breathed in life, feeling a tremendous mixture of hope, gratitude, and fear. *Please, Lord, let me love this boy as much as I loved my Chloe.* As if to reassure me, Karen said, "He loves people. It shouldn't surprise me that my dogs always seem to go to the right owners."

I could only imagine how little Levi must have felt, having been abruptly stolen away from his siblings and the only home he'd ever known. Following the trauma of the first car ride, I sat vigil as my eight-week-old bundle passed out on the kitchen floor. Then he lifted up his sweet head, fixed those big brown puppy eyes on the face of his kidnapper, threw back his head and let me have it. I didn't even know he was old enough to bark. Was this normal?

As you may recall, I have had no children to practice on, and this was my first puppy. I was not prepared. I pictured soft, sweet, and snugly. Instead, I seemed to have acquired some kind of gorgon who wanted to poison me with his little baby fangs.

I spent hours online looking up puppy temperaments with searches like, "Is my puppy aggressive?" "How to stop puppy biting before it's too late," and "Puppy buyer's remorse." I bonded with The Dog Whisperer, but Cesar's corrective *"chhtt!"* sound would never work for me.

At least housebreaking wasn't difficult. I knew enough not to punish, and Levi learned quickly. I kept him barricaded in the kitchen—since the floor isn't pretty—for potty accidents, play, and to keep myself safe. I remember trying to walk from the back door to the dining room, which required going through the kitchen. There he was, facing me squarely, coiled and ready to pounce on my ankles. Spotting a dentist bill on the edge of the counter, I sailed it into the room. He attacked the envelope, while I escaped, unbloodied, safely through to the other side.

A friend risked a pandemic visit to meet Levi. Seeing my haggard expression, she exclaimed, "Oh my goodness, are you alright? Did somebody die?" *Just my rose-colored dreams of an idyllic puppyhood,* I thought.

Anxious to greet my boy, she stepped over the baby gate and directly into the kitchen war zone. Before I could stop her, she'd kicked off her sandals and exposed her defenseless little toes. Levi spent the rest of the visit crated, and I spent it apologizing.

The internet possesses the diabolical skill of offering us a hundred small solutions, while at the same time promoting every possible catastrophe. YouTube may exploit our darkest fears, but oh what peace we often forfeit, all because we do not realize that puppies do, in fact, grow up.

In April of 2021, I received my first call-back from a nursing home. After explaining about Chloe, I introduced Levi, and at eight months old, we took our first tentative steps.

The one brilliant thing I had done, thanks be to God, was introduce him to the stroller on his first night. He slept in it like a pram beside the bed, zipped up and tucked away, and it became his second home for our first month together. But that didn't mean I knew how he'd do at work.

We began in the dayroom, and when the administrator appeared in the doorway to welcome us, Levi tossed back his head and let him have it. But rather than merit his first bad review, young Mr. Levi brought down the house like a seasoned pro. In his exuberance he threw himself at the residents and licked every finger and nose in sight. Funniest thing, no one expected a puppy to be perfect. He could do no wrong. He said "I love you" and "God bless you," just like his big sister had, adorned in her yellow bandana which was too big but made him all the more adorable. Levi hadn't yet been groomed and looked like a rag mop, the old-fashioned kind made of dreadnought cotton. You could barely see his eyes. He was an immediate star.

Since our first Thanksgiving night he's been on my bed. He curls up tightly, pushes himself against my side and sighs. If I cry, he washes my face. Residents and staff have been known to kiss him smack on the mouth. In idle moments we take turns chasing each other around the house—I may as well be on my honeymoon.

Who's a good boy?

33

The Judgment

While my car was being broken into in my own driveway at two in the morning, I was snoring softly in my little bed with my tiny watchdog paddling in his dreams beside me.

Those thieves broke in, not just to steal, but to do a lot of damage. A few days after the tow truck, the rental car, and the insurance inspection, I found myself sobbing in the den and missing my deceased parents for the first time in years. Missing the parents who'd hurt me, who were hurt themselves, who didn't know how to take care of me. Never mind what kind of parents they'd been. Suddenly I felt so vulnerable.

Parental love is supposed to be a given. But families just don't come with a guarantee.

I have a friend who grew up securely loved. She finds it easy to love people, too. She speaks of love as if it were as organically attached to family life as jelly is devoted to peanut butter. She has always rested deeply in love like it's a big, overstuffed chair with her name on it. She raises her arms, closes her eyes, and falls backwards into it at the end of the day knowing she will be caught, cared for, and kept safe.

Others of us come home, sit down, and fall right on our you-know-whats because, while we were out, someone moved the furniture. And someone keeps moving it, so we never know where it will be next. We just go on skinning our shins in the dark. Like that old joke, you go to camp when you're eight years old and come home to find your parents have changed the locks. But it's not funny.

Children deserve to be entirely protected. In a perfect world, parents would surround them all with strength, power, and love. And no matter the decades that have passed, a great part of me refuses to let that ideal go. When destruction happens, I'm always eight years old.

My nursing home friend Gary once used that word "destruction" in describing the facility where he lives. I had just sung him my "Creation Song" while he lay there wiggling his toes in time and tapping imaginary drums on his blanket.

> *And God said, "Let there be light,"*
> *And it was light*
> *And God called the darkness "Night"*
> *And it was night*
> *There was evening,*
> *There was morning*
> *On the first day…*
> *And the stars sang in the heavens*
> *And He rested on day seven*
> *Then He blessed what He had made,*
> *And God said…*
> *"It was good!"*
> –Susan Piper, "Creation Song," *God Is*

"Creation theory, creation, that's good," he said. I piped in that God is our Master Creator and re-Creator as well. "We need that around here," he continued. "We just have destruction. We don't have any love, there's just destruction. People are dying all over the place."

It was a sad summary indeed. Gary really knows suffering. I'm not sure he knows the Lord, but I try to talk to him as if he does. He's been bed-bound in that place for years. He's fairly young, using myself as the standard. Young for a nursing home, at least. I've always thought of him like a brother.

Gary went to church as a child and knows some Scripture. "I think I heard somewhere that sin is the cause of sickness and death. The wages of sin, something like that. In college I remember thinking if I could just get rid of more sin, then more sickness would go away." He looked at me to see what I would say.

I backed him up. Romans 6:23, *The wages of sin is death*, confirmed the association with sickness and every destructive thing. But rather than go into details of correlation I stuck to the subject of suffering and offered to him the glorious end of the children of God. With a body like his, he was ready to think of a new one. And as for the present pain, I quoted my very late Puritan boyfriend Matthew Henry who wrote, "God takes the evil out of the affliction of His children." He liked that. Gary repeated it, looking at me sideways, since he couldn't move his neck. "God takes the evil out. That's good."

Before I offer God's hope and future to anyone, I always try to interject the necessity of faith in Christ. Gary brought up the lesson of the sheep and the goats, which gave our conversation a natural transition into the difference between who belongs to God and who doesn't. He spoke like a sheep. I spoke like I believed him.

I have spent some time studying that very passage in Matthew 25:31-46. As someone raised under the cruel eye of perfection, I am keenly aware of my inability to reach the bar of requirements that justice demands. Most always, that throws me back onto the bosom of my loving Savior and I am helped. But when I am reminded of "standing before the Lord in judgment," I am likely to forget to look at Him and see only myself. Which is not a good perspective in the Christian life.

My stomach has always turned at the prospect of being judged, whether by God or man. I once made the mistake of asking for someone's opinion, forgetting myself and imagining I was a person who could grow and learn by "constructive criticism." What sailed back at me was an off-the-cuff response with something very hard and cold up its sleeve. It sent me flying onto my you-know what, and I stayed down for a good two days.

I have wrestled with the various interpretations of the Last Judgment for years. On one occasion I heard a leader in a respected denomination declare, "Good works are necessary for salvation!" He was emphatic. I waited for him to explain that he meant they necessarily follow after, as evidence, not prerequisite. But he never said a blinkin' word.

There's a lot of talk of trembling on the internet. Little-known and high-profile pastors alike warn that some will be saved by the skin of their teeth while their sins are paraded in public for everyone to see. But aren't those the sins God promises to remember no more? Aren't we the ones who, because we look to Him, will never be ashamed?

How does the paradigm shift from singing "I Need Thee Every Hour" in life to God answering "What have you done for Me lately" in death?

"Not What My Hands Have Done." I thought that was obvious.

Now, here comes a bright someone who will mention the motivation of rewards. He might even be from your church. But he forgets his audience. Any reference to a rewards system, even a heavenly one, fills me with competition and panic. Lord knows I should be canvassing the neighborhood with salvation tracts instead of sitting in my basement den watching detective shows every night. My candle predictably goes out about eight o'clock p.m. I guess my mansion will look like a room in the Southside Strip Mall Motel.

It seems to me that churches present different renderings for the Day of Reckoning. Some promote fear and trembling, while others predict a future so nicely sewn up that the congregation can snore softly in their pews with nary a collective doubt. If that's your church, you're probably thinking, "What in the world is she so worried about? Why doesn't she just join our denomination?"

But whether we have been pulled off the streets by the scruff of our necks or nurtured from the day of our birth, we must all agree: the world is broken.

Really, badly, broken.

Regardless of denominational divides or if we have or haven't faith in Christ, we only need to look around to see faces, hearts, bodies, lives—all groaning together under the curse pronounced by God Himself. Our earnings of death have been collecting interest since Genesis, Chapter 3.

I can't reconcile giving my Savior an account of my life with the fact that He already knows it all. What reward is mine for doing what He ordained and gave me His Spirit to accomplish? What can be taken from me because of my failings which He's already covered in His blood?

I think the biggest stumbling block before me is that this cataclysmic event *is* before me. Even the most mature believer is peering into a glass darkly. The staunchest defender of "Scripture alone!" must admit a certain amount of conjecture, of connecting the jots and tittles to formulate a picture of how all this will ultimately play out. Maybe you won't mind if I share a little sanctified imagining of my own.

I see Him now. The rising of the Great Day reveals Him as He is, and in His light I can see who I've become. I am covered in broidered gold and white linen, and I am shining as the stars in the heavens, as a precious jewel in the crown of the King. I am so overwhelmed by His joy in presenting me that I can hardly contain myself.

See, on His left, our Abuser and his minions are going down to the singing of the multitudes of angels and saints. Shouts of "Hallelujah!" leap from every breast as destruction and wickedness go up in smoke. I am surrounded by strength, power, and love; I am aware of being entirely protected for the first time in my life. I know whom I have believed, and His is the voice that speaks to me now, saying, "Do you know what this is? This is The Judgment."

Now unto him that is able to keep you from falling, and to present you faultless before the presence of his glory with exceeding joy, To the only wise God our Savior, be glory and majesty, dominion and power, both now and ever. Amen.

Jude 24-25

34

Second-Chance Roses

My next-door neighbors are ideal. We have no fences between us, and they are so thoughtful I would never want one. We exchange dessert overages and keep an eye out when one of us goes away. The husband on one side even mows my lawn sometimes, and when my precious little Chloe died, he came with a shovel and helped me dig. I didn't even have to ask.

Farther down the block, it's a different story at the tiny, run-down home of a family of six. I've sometimes wished I could sneak out at midnight to wrap a huge fence around the trash cans and leaves those folks often forget to clean up.

But because I belong to Christ, I have always tried to initiate exchanges with that overflowing family, even over the leaves and cans. We would chat a bit, coming and going, but had never gotten past that. I invited them twice to open-house gatherings, but they never came and never said why.

Until one afternoon there was a knock on my door. There stood that very leaf-mom from down the street, with my umbrella in her hand.

"Did you drop this? I found it in the driveway."

Indeed, I had dropped my big orange umbrella that I carry while walking my new little puppy, to protect us from rain and unleashed big dogs that run at us with their hair standing up. ("He won't hurt you; he just wants to *play*.") I was glad to have my defense-weapon back and thanked her. She looked past me into the living room while we made small talk, but I didn't invite her in. And she was gone.

It was the first time she'd ever knocked. Why didn't I ask her in? The perfect outreach opportunity had been handed to me, and I'd dropped it, just like the umbrella. I didn't know what my problem was.

Feeling some serious regret, I talked to the Lord.

Have you ever asked the Lord for a specific second chance? I did once, long ago, and He gave it to me. So I asked Him to please bring my neighbor back again.

A week later, on the Saturday before Mother's Day, someone was on my stoop. Puppy Levi was barking. "Is that my neighbor?" I asked, running past the door for my pink baseball cap to hide my messy hair, thinking I was addressing my good-mowing friend.

"Yes…"

Looking through the window I saw not my next-door neighbor, but the busy mother of four standing there, holding six long-stemmed red roses. I threw the door open. "Evelyn, please come in! Please sit down! I am so happy to see you!"

Perched on the edge of my sofa in her BJ's Wholesale Club T-shirt, Evelyn began to explain. "We were given these at work and I thought, 'What am I going to do with roses?' And you flashed through my mind."

"Oh no, listen, it was the Lord, I have been praying! I felt so sorry when you knocked before and I didn't ask you in. I said, 'Lord, why didn't I ask her in?' and I've been praying for a second chance. You are the answer to my prayers. He put me on your mind!"

We had the nicest visit, so warm and neighborly. Levi was excited to meet her on his own turf and didn't even nip in his puppy joy. "He's so good!" my neighbor exclaimed. She even liked my Goodwill furniture, so we had a tour of the house. I don't have very many visitors, and Evelyn was so complimentary about my eclectic decorating style that it gave me a real boost. I packed up some homemade carrot cake for her to take home to her family, and she left.

Then I sat down and cried.

I am not a nice person. That is not false humility, that's the truth. I am also not a mother, and Mother's Day traditionally has delivered an emotional wallop that takes me days to get over; from my own sad relationship with my late mother to the fact that I am nearly a senior citizen with no progeny excepting the new little puppy.

It was in "raising" Levi that I was reminded that I truly am not a nice person. Like I needed a reminder. But my sin does much more than spoil my disposition; according to God, it makes me an actual criminal. I do not love Him as I should, and I clearly don't love my neighbor (nor my puppy) as myself.

I know, too, that my Heavenly Father has given me grace, undeserved by my criminal nature, and He walks with me, talks with me, and tells me I am His own.

How amazingly kind of God to send Evelyn to my door again after my first botched opportunity. That was all I'd asked for, and that was more than enough.

But on top of that, there were roses. Not just any roses, but Mother's Day roses, specifically marked out for the occasion and hand-delivered to me by one of the hard-working women at BJ's.

Looking back, it seems to me that if I had done what a good Christian should have done, and invited my neighbor in the first time she'd knocked, I would not have had the faith-growing answer to prayer that God graciously provided. She still might have returned with the roses, but they wouldn't have meant as much to me.

Jesus didn't come to call the righteous to repentance. It's in God's forgiveness of sin that He exalts and crowns His graciousness, for His own glory. This is His heart-warming and love-inspiring, long-stemmed, Mother's Day roses-to-the-barren-soul grace. See how He shows off His beauty and extols His passion by not only laying down His life to cleanse His bride, but by rising from the dead to dress her in His own spotless garment. And then, bending down to give her roses.

Marvelous grace of our loving Lord,
Grace that exceeds our sin and our guilt!
Yonder on Calvary's mount out-poured—
There where the blood of the Lamb was spilt.
–Julia H. Johnston, 1910

35

Wine

I really can do without fancy dinners.

But it is lovely to be welcomed to such affairs, so when some Christian friends invited me to one, I accepted.

Standing beside their glittering dining room table, I caught sight of the host picking up the telltale bottle in the kitchen. My senses, by reason of overuse, were exercised years ago to spot such things. I'm surprised I couldn't smell it from where I was standing.

"You know none for me, right?" I reminded him. "Yes, but you don't mind if we imbibe, do you?" he asked, displaying the label in the crook of his arm.

I had to lie. I was in their home. It was their right, and as a guest, I felt I had to say I didn't mind. What would you have done?

Maybe we could call it a partial truth. Because "I didn't mind" as long as I didn't have to hear everyone compliment the vintage, describe the fruitiness, watch it swirl around in everyone's glass but mine, smell it, hear the satisfied "*Ah...*" that followed each taste—it was all okay by me. I didn't mind if they drank to drunkenness as long as I wasn't there to be tempted by it. I mean, maybe I could suggest they not get drunk out of Christian concern, but that was as far as I would go.

But all the rest, I really did mind, in truth. And I also didn't think they showed much concern themselves, to do all that in front of me. They know I'm not just on some sobriety kick. They know the Lord removed alcohol from me in a beautiful, grace-filled and program-less gesture soon after my conversion, but not until I'd already been a secret drunk since my teens.

Well, none of us have perfect friends, and I need to remember I'm not one either. But I have One Perfect Friend, so I took my heart to Him the next day in my devotional time. I reported what He already knew, along with a bit of complaining, and asked Him what I should think, how I should feel about these things.

I opened to Song of Solomon and read, *He brought me into the banqueting house, and his banner over me was love* (Song of Solomon 2:4). *Yes*, I thought, *You invite me to a feast, don't you, Lord?* and I felt comforted. He wouldn't treat me thoughtlessly at *His* feast.

When I go to my freezing-in-winter and boiling-in-summer sun porch in the morning to pray, I take my Bible, my journal, my puppy, my coffee, and my big, old fashioned, hard-bound Strong's Concordance. It's an actual book. It weighs a ton. It should; it's full of truth. I love looking things up.

I looked up "banqueting," expecting to find a feast described. But no food was mentioned there: H3196, *yayin* from an unused root meaning to *effervesce*; wine (as fermented); by implication intoxication: banqueting, wine, winebibber.

He brought me to the house of wine! Now here, if I were a less sophisticated person, is where I would insert a smiley face. And it isn't just intoxication to which He brings me; He flies a conspicuous flag of love over me at the same time. My Beloved can be quite ostentatious when He has a mind to be.

I followed the "wine" theme around a bit in the Holy Romance Book and came to this: *Let him kiss me with the kisses of his mouth: for thy love is better than wine* (Song of Solomon 1:2). More extravagant love to satisfy my soul. Now I picked up my other devotional help, my cell phone, where the internet keeps the commentaries—the thoughts of ancient, learned men. These men like to think. Too much thinking, sometimes, I think. But I consult them and know that they must know a lot more than I, even though I am still stubborn enough to argue. They can't hear me.

So, somebody, in fact more than one somebody, came up with the thought that actually a certain verb should be turned this way and not that way, and the aforementioned "Let him kiss me" sentence (were they uncomfortable with kissing?) should really read: "Give me to drink." Interesting. Where have we heard that theme before?

There cometh a woman of Samaria to draw water: Jesus saith unto her...if thou knewest the gift of God...thou wouldest have asked of him, and he would have given thee living water (John 4:7, 10).

Ah...can you taste that? Living water, offered like a kiss of forgiveness to a desperate woman, filling her soul like her own personal well. Never thirsty anymore, could it be? Never again resorting to the same sinful habits, shamed by the heat of the sun, despairing to find what she'd been missing all her life? *"Let him give me to drink, for thy love is better...."* Can you hear her as the realization dawns? *"Sir, give me this water, that I thirst not, neither come hither to draw! Fly that banner of love over me!"*

My Lord answered me on my porch that morning. He told me what I should think and what I should feel about these things. No need to mourn the lesser wine, the lesser friends, the lesser feasts and loves. You can set that open bottle in front of me; I will not gaze upon it. That which is perfect has come, and I am not thirsty anymore.

*"Or leave a kiss but in the cup,
and I'll not ask for wine."*
–Ben Johnson, 1616

36

Oil

...I shall be anointed with fresh oil.
Psalms 92:10

I am of a certain age. I don't think I need to be specific. Let's just say I am not a bird of spring anymore. And I've been single for a long time. I'm used to it. I don't often think "that way" about men anymore. I guess I've outgrown romance. My apologies if you're a man.

I know I'm aging outside; there's not much I can do about that. But because of this "certain age," I went to the doctor for routine blood work, to see how I'm aging inside. Turns out, not only has Christ made my soul sweeter, but some of that sweetness must have leached into my blood. The results showed pre-diabetes.

I took action and quickly cut way back on carbs and sugar. Consequently, I lost thirty pounds. Which made my face look older, but let my body fit into clothes I've also outgrown. I was pretty happy about that.

Soon after, I took my slenderized self to visit my missionary friend Myriam, who presented me with a box of clothing she'd collected from the donation room in the basement of her apartment building. It was like Christmas. And the best thing was, everything fit. Blouses, jeans, and one pair of rather tight white pants. The kind "they" are wearing right now.

"Myriam, are these too immodest?" I asked, modeling them for her.

"They're fine!" she replied.

I'm not arguing with Myriam, but to the pure, all things are pure.

I felt pretty proud and snappy in those pants. "Snappy" is an age-defining word. You would never use it, I'm sure. I wore them to my afternoon nursing home, and then around the block with Levi.

If I don't wear clothes for a full eight hours, I will sometimes hang them up as soon as I come home and wear them again the next day. Besides, I really liked those pants. So, Day Two. Same block, same pants. Up pulled my neighbor from one street over and rolled down his window. Leaning out he said, "I saw you yesterday and I said, 'She knows she looks good in those white pants!'"

I started to explain. *Just be practical, he just needs the facts.* "Oh, I got some blood work done, and my sugar was high, so I cut back on carbs and sugar and I lost weight, and then a friend gave me these pants. But you're a married man, I don't think your wife would like you talking about these things," I said, babbling and smiling and nodding. I know I was smiling. Uncomfortable, but entirely flattered and smiling. So much for getting over romance.

"I can still look, can't I? Nothing wrong with looking!" he insisted.

"Well, you're a married man, and I'm a Christian, so, better stop now, God bless, 'bye!" (I really did say, "God bless." It didn't help.)

He drove away and I immediately began to think of what I'd said and felt. I knew, before God, that my words were not nearly as discouraging as they should have been, and I'd messed up. I started to pray. I took a different way home just so I wouldn't pass his house. But ten minutes later I heard a car behind me. "Beep-beep! beep-beep!" I knew it was him. I just kept walking.

I have a sinful history with men. I've been chaste for over twenty years, but I'm not quite as sanctified as I thought. The dog returns to his vomit (Proverbs 26:11) and just one little nudge was all it took to turn me, too. I let it sink in and spent the evening repenting.

As God and YouTube would have it, up popped an evangelical man-on-the-street outreach film that occupied the rest of my night and gave me a break from repeating myself to the Lord. Real people being convinced by an ace apologist (and the Holy Spirit) that God is real and they have a reason to live. I watched faces turn from sharp self-satisfaction to the soft, openness of hope. From their own vomit to heavenly bread, we could say, if we didn't mind being so graphic.

The next day, wearing different pants of course, I drove to my local mechanic for an oil change. Frank came recommended by our pastor. The first time I met him, he announced, "I used to be Christian but now I'm Catholic." That was an interesting confession.

I called him on my way because his road was under construction. I would have to find another way around, so I'd be a little late. His brother answered the phone.

"He doesn't have the oil," he said. "It didn't come in. Do you want to make it another day?"

Well, no, I didn't, because I'd hurried already and had a busy schedule. I heard the clang of a heavy curse word dropping in the background.

"Is he angry with me for still coming?" I asked.

"No, he's just having a bad day. Someone will go for the oil. You can still come in."

In I came. It was ninety degrees in that garage. "You can sit there, it's clean," Frank's brother directed. I was happy to sit, but even happier that my pants were now blue.

The back-and-forth chatter between the technicians related to sex with under-aged girls and the consequences. They were following a news story on the big-screen TV. From the stool beside me, a young customer chimed in on the conversation, his face glued to a video on his phone. The star on his screen had much to say, every other word substituted with *bleep! bleep!*

"Is this someone you admire?" I asked him.

"No," he said, never taking his eyes away.

It was a squirming experience and I didn't enjoy it. I did some praying sitting there, aware of the "I Work for God" sign on my dashboard and my responsibility to represent Christ, the failure of the previous afternoon still fresh on my mind.

Frank ran my credit card through, then sat down just as I stood up to go.

"Pray for me," he began. "It's been a real bad week. Two days ago my dad died all of a sudden. We knew he had congestive heart failure, but the doctor had given him five years. He didn't take his medicine. And now they think I have Parkinson's. Look at my hand." It was shaking. He continued, "I always try to help people. I guess things happen for a purpose...."

Poor Frank. While I was expressing sympathy and assuring him of my and my church's prayers, out of the blue he said, "You know what always got me? The Trinity. How could the Son who was always the Son become the Son when he was born?"

And we were off.

I tried to explain the mystery of the incarnation; God took humanity to Himself by becoming the God-man.

"God doesn't change, right?" I reminded him. "The Son is and was always the Son."

I shared that Christ had to become a man to keep the law perfectly in our place. That His righteousness is ours through faith, and He died as a man to pay for our sins. It was simply the gospel, just the incredible purpose of God. "Like you said, Frank, God does things for a purpose," I repeated.

Then I asked, "What do you like about the Catholic church?"

"I like the history of it, you know?" he answered.

"You said you used to be Christian?" It was a brazen question, but I was quoting.

"Oh, I was raised Christian, we went to all kinds of Christian churches, especially the one on the east side for a long time," Frank explained.

"Did that church teach you that it's not about what you do, but about what Christ has done?"

There I was, woman-not-on-the street but in the grimy garage, with no microphone, no cameras, just the power of the Holy Spirit working through my still-sinful self. Not my own, but the gracious words of Christ were falling, spilling over into the lap of this hard-working, sad and searching man.

"You can find it all in your Bible," I encouraged him, as I shook his other hand.

"Oh, I have plenty of those," he nodded.

I drove away to the grocery store full of joy and power, my head held very high. Since I had run into my "I can still look" neighbor in that store before, I hoped he might be there today. I was ready for him. I practiced as I drove, picturing my bold approach in the produce section. "I have something to say," I'd tell him. "I want to apologize for not discouraging you when you spoke to me yesterday from your car. As a Christian, I did the wrong thing. I mean no offense; you're my neighbor and I want to live at peace with you. But I am asking you please to never speak to me that way again about the way I look. I will appreciate that and so will your wife."

Take words with you, and return to the LORD.
Say to Him,
"Take away all iniquity;
Receive us graciously:
For we will offer the sacrifices of our lips."
Hosea 14:2 NKJV

37
Whom Have I?

Whom have I in heaven but thee?
Psalms 73:25

During a discussion on the Lord's Supper one Sunday, some helpful person mentioned the dire consequences of Christians who come to the table in an "unworthy manner." This alarming suggestion of discipline disturbed me greatly and sent me running to my Bible. Reading the passage in I Corinthians disturbed me even more.

For he that eateth and drinketh unworthily, eateth and drinketh damnation to himself, not discerning the Lord's body. For this cause many are weak and sickly among you, and many sleep (1 Corinthians 11:29-30).

I'd read it many times before, but this time the passage struck me with fear. The man who had brought it up at church implied that we must all make great preparations for the supper *or else*. That made my wounded conscience break out in a cold sweat. God will kill me if I'm not well-enough prepared?

I'm no Bible scholar, but after that day I really delved into the passage. Sadly, according to the commentaries of the pious and deceased men whom I revere, I discovered I'm alone in thinking the "sleeping" (killed) ones weren't real Christians. But let me explain my reasoning.

You understand, death for a Christian is a step up to glory. "Far better," according to Paul. Granted, it would have been shocking to see people dropping over at communion. But what kind of warning whisks believers away to glory? It seems to me that God was making examples of riotous unbelievers, so that everyone, especially His children, would discern between vulgar gluttony and the spiritual presence of His crucified, incarnate Son. I think the sleepers were the spots in the love feasts that Jude talks about (Jude 1:12). But I'm no scholar, and really, folks don't listen to me.

From what I can tell, the closest I've come to a discipline-from-God scenario occurred when I tried to buy my first house. I had three thousand dollars (which I'd borrowed from a brother in the Lord) as a down payment. I had thoughtlessly thrown down one thousand as earnest money on a house I didn't even like, thinking it would be good enough. I certainly didn't pray about my decision.

Then my dog Chloe got really, really sick; sick enough to almost die.

I had to rush her to the emergency vet on New Year's Eve. That would be a holiday. That would cost another thousand dollars. And they didn't even do anything out of the ordinary, just tests and fluids. As I wrote the check I thought, *There goes my down payment.*

It immediately became clear to me that the Lord did not want me to buy that "good enough" house. He had stopped me in my tracks. A wave of dread swept over me as I realized I'd done wrong. I hadn't even consulted God concerning a major life decision. For a while I was afraid to even look for another house.

But in God's mercy, I got my money back (from the realtor, not the vet) and more importantly, dear Chloe survived. God had been firm, but He also showed me His kindness.

So why had I become so afraid of God?

Once the dust had settled, I began to see my reaction as the reminiscent after-shock of trauma. Since childhood, the experience of being blind-sided by betrayal has been deeply embedded in my brain. Back when my mother handed my diary to the school board and they fired the teacher I adored, my "trusted" parent suddenly became my enemy. Now, through the lens of my failed house-buying panic, I was seeing God as my enemy, too.

It's the suddenness of trauma that shakes you, the shock of the unexpected, the awful event you can never be prepared for—like that threat of sudden judgment at the Lord's Supper. That particular threat may have sent me on a researching frenzy, but I soon discovered I'm not the only trembling soul in the world.

My internet searches of the killing-at-the-table verse had revealed multitudes of Christians concerned that God might strike them dead. Each scholarly reply confirmed that Scripture was indeed giving such a warning. One helpful well-known gentleman suggested that God was *saving believers from hell* by "bringing them home." (I must have misinterpreted the entire Bible. I thought the cross had already saved me from hell.) I finally found one still, small voice that supported my argument that God doesn't need to "discipline" us that way today. The blogger was a trauma survivor.

To the heart that knows abuse, understanding Scripture is more than an intellectual exercise. Scholars may have the luxury of postulating from the backs of high horses, from the safety of God-would-never-do-this-to-us. It's like they know too much to fear that kind of fear. The rest of us broken hearts are down here in the dirt, praying we won't get stepped on. Praying what we do know is enough.

But it's not the scholar's knowledge that makes him safe. It's the character of God.

Jack, one of my nursing home regulars, has many of his own reasons to mistrust God. And he isn't shy about sharing them. Instead of saying hello, he sometimes greets me with "I CAN'T believe in God, I just CAN'T believe in God, it doesn't make sense! Science has proven it!" And I stand there, letting him hit me with bullet after bullet of machine-gunned questions he thinks he is the first to think of, right down to Adam and Eve's children marrying each other. Then I ask permission to speak.

I try to address his arguments. Some are easily answered. Others, I would need my own degree in science to resolve. But this dear man doesn't really need data or research or archeology. His heart is broken. He has MS, cancer of the bladder and the prostate, and he's angry and afraid.

Levi, my munchkin-of-a-ministry partner, touches Jack's heart. A darling little buffer he is. Jack likes to tease him by making circles in the air with treats while Levi follows him with his nose. Jack pretends to eat them first. He talks to Levi, never mentioning God.

Levi talks too, and must always bark "I love you!" before we go.

"I will leave you with one question, Jack, for you to ponder. Where does love come from?"

"Love comes from God," he answers without even thinking. Then he abruptly looks up at me.

"You tricked me," he says.

Through the lens of his anger and illness-driven fear, Jack sees me as an enemy who fooled him into confessing the truth. But I don't have that kind of power. It's out of the abundance of the heart that the mouth speaks (Matthew 12:34). Jack's brain may be telling him he can't trust God. His wounded heart hopes otherwise.

As much as I would love to coax Jack into the kingdom of God and win you scholars to my interpretation of Scripture, I know I'll never convince a soul of anything. But neither will I relinquish my understanding of the Hand that holds my own. I have to be able to run to the Lord or I will have nothing, absolutely nothing, to cling to. If He closes His arms to me, I really will die. I think that's in the Bible, too.

I will never be well-enough prepared. But I lay me down on the truth that a bruised reed He will not break. God may not be predictable, but He is also not capricious. He has no use for manipulation or power plays. God loves believers as He loves His Son, but He already knows what's in a man. He doesn't need to "bring us home" because He can't trust us down here anymore. He doesn't trust us at all. He trusts Himself. Therein lies my peace.

There is no fear in love,
but perfect love casts out fear.
For fear has to do with punishment,
and whoever fears has not been perfected in love.
I John 4:18 ESV

38

This Little Light of Mine

There's nothing small about James.

I don't mean his size, although he's still quite tall for 92, having retained much of his health, his only "helpers" being a rolling walker and hearing aids. But he's the most expressive man I've ever met.

Because of his hearing loss, he's also loud, which adds to the drama. But his is no melodrama. He is overwhelmingly sincere.

Visiting James is an immersive experience, like a movie in an interactive theater with shaking seats and surround sound. There is no escaping once you're in his presence. And for reasons unknown, he's full of love for me.

He will shout me into his room, waving his arms as he beckons and jumping up to move his sweater off the chair so I can sit down. Then he will begin.

Ninety-two years' worth of memories make his stories very long. I try to track with him, but I confess I lose my way if he retraces back to his great-grandmother. All the women in James' life were strong, including his wife. She died a year ago, and he remains as passionate about her as he is about everything else. He still hears her voice every night, "Don't forget the light, James."

But even if I lose my place in his stories, I can never lose sight of James. His eyes grow wide, his head tilts back, his arms are in constant motion, he laughs and cries in the same sentence. If he were only younger, I would throw myself at him and ask him to marry me and make me as alive as he is for the rest of my life. I always stay too long. I can't bear to leave him.

"I haven't thought of these things in years! Nobody here knows these things"—waving towards the door— "I don't know how I got started; I don't know why they all came to my mind today." His eyes are shining.

"They're not a secret, are they, James?"

He laughs.

"I can't help but notice," I tell him, "that your life is an amazing example of God's faithfulness. It reminds me of a hymn." And I begin to sing:

> *All the way my Savior leads me,*
> *What have I to ask beside?*
> *Can I doubt His tender mercies,*
> *Who through life has been my guide?*

James sits frozen in his chair, his hand to his open mouth. He's looking past me, staring straight ahead, as if he's been tasered and stunned into stiffness.

I sing two verses, the only ones I really know. He turns to me slowly, his crescendos now compressed, his decibel levels subdued.

"This can't be an accident that you came here today. I can't tell you what your being here...what you have offered for my faith. I don't know what to say. I can't thank you enough." His eyes are red as he reaches towards me. "Can I touch you?"

I stand and offer my hand; he pulls it to his face, presses it against his cheek and closes his eyes. "Thank you," he whispers. I tell him how much Levi and I love him, and we go.

Now, this is not an average nursing home visit, but it is typical of an encounter with dear James. Do you think I deserve this kind of appreciation? Did I do something so marvelous and unique for him? Do you know who I am? I'll remind you.

I'm the moon. I mentioned this in an early chapter about my mother, where I explained that as a child I existed to reflect her and had no personhood of my own. I was nothing then, and on my own I'm nothing still. I'm just the moon.

The moon changes constantly, waxing and waning, brilliant one day and a dirty fingernail in the sky the next. But the moon was made to reflect the sun, and therein lies its value. It all depends on whom you are reflecting.

We are all so weak. We're all a mess, you must know that. So you know it wasn't I who touched the tender and passionate heart of James. It's true that I can sing and play an instrument, although as I've also mentioned before, it's surprising that I can, because I'm very clumsy. I'm the person who drops the eggs in the grocery store. Literally.

Thankfully it was only half a dozen, but they went rolling and cracking to the feet of another very big man, who squatted with his hands stretched out like a child, frantically grabbing and trying to catch them. It was much too late, but his efforts on my behalf were endearing.

"Sir, thank you so much! I'm so sorry. Why don't you just put them in the empty carton on the floor so they'll all be together and I'll call someone to clean up my mess."

He stood up, towering over me. "I know you, I'm your neighbor."

So he was, the son of an older man down the street who always seemed to be on his front porch before the pandemic, waiting for Chloe and me to go by on our walks.

"Oh! Sure, how's your father?"

He shook his head. "He's doin' bad. He's declining. He just sits in front of the TV and he won't see anybody, not even his sister. I live in the basement. My nephew lives there too, and he's not"—he searched for the word— "respective of anybody. He's bad."

"Oh, he doesn't treat you or your parents with respect?"

"No, I've tried, there's nothing anybody can do."

"Well, you can pray, God answers prayers." I pointed up towards the fluorescent lights on the ceiling.

"Yeah, but I don't go to church."

"You don't have to be in the garage to be a car, you know." I wasn't worried about downplaying church. If he came to Christ, Christ would take him there.

"Yeah, I never thought of it that way." He was smiling.

I went on, "I used to think that I had to do good things to get God to love me, but I knew I wasn't good enough for God and that He would know the truth...." Pausing only to wave approaching carts away from the mess I'd made, I shared Christ in the dairy aisle with my neighbor's son, while he wiped away the tears.

God's people were created to manifest Christ. Broken as the eggs, unstable as the moon, it makes no never mind to God. John the Baptist said, "I must decrease and He must increase," but Jesus called him a "burning and a shining light." I know who John was. John was the moon. Thanks be to God, I know who I am and what I was made for, too.

I sing the songs and drop the eggs.

Let your light so shine before men, that they may see your good works and glorify your Father which is in heaven.
Matthew 5:16

39

Death and Life

Some dog trainers say you should never let your dog sleep with you because it will make him think he's your equal. Although I am struggling to control my very smart and strong-willed pup, he's in the bed for my sake, not his. I just couldn't sleep if he weren't there. He, on the other hand, would probably be fine.

One Good Friday night he was restless and making lots of snuffling noises, so neither of us was sleeping. When he finally quieted down I got nervous, putting my hand on his little belly to make sure he was still breathing, which of course he was. But I was remembering our visit with Karl in assisted living that very afternoon.

I had pulled up a chair beside Karl's big lounger, maneuvering Levi's stroller carefully to avoid the long green oxygen tube coiled all around Karl's feet. He has eight children, so I knew it was safe to ask about his Easter plans.

"Karl, you'll see some of your kids over the weekend, won't you?"

"My daughter and son-in-law are picking me up at eight tomorrow."

"Wow, eight in the morning on a Saturday, that's an early start. What's on your agenda?"

"We'll visit the graves. My wife, my parents, my two sons, my brothers and sisters, my cousins...."

"Karl, I didn't know you'd lost two sons. I am so sorry, that must have been terrible. I know you have many living children, and I'm sure that doesn't take away your loss or pain, but I'm so glad you do have them. They must be a comfort, at least, for you; do you know what I mean?"

He took a breath. "Karl Junior was four months old. I decided he was old enough to sleep in the bed with us for a special occasion, so I went down the hall to get him. He was black and blue. I ran screaming down the stairs and to the neighbor's because they had a phone. The police came, the fire department came." He was staring straight ahead.

"Oh, no...was it sudden infant death syndrome?" I asked quietly.

"I don't know," shaking his head.

He didn't mention how he'd lost his other son. We just sat for a few moments.

Finally I asked, "Well, I have some hymns about the resurrection, may I sing one for you? Do you have any favorites?"

"We don't have those in our church. No offense."

In my opinion, if someone says "no offense," it means there probably is a reason to be offended. Similarly, if you tell me, "I'm not judging you," I have a sneaking suspicion you are. In this case, I think Karl was implying that his denomination's hymns were theologically superior to mine. ...*Stand by thyself, come not near to me; for I am holier than thou* (Isaiah 65:5).

What could possibly be superior to the resurrection of Christ our Lord?

"Oh, okay, but do you like "How Great Thou Art"? They sing that in your church." He agreed.

I didn't get through the first line. He burst into tears, sobbing while the oxygen tube shook sympathetically in his poor, misshapen cauliflower nose.

Putting the guitar down, I picked up Levi. "Here, Levi, you visit Uncle Karl now." Levi was not happy about being pushed into Karl's lap, but he submitted under a steady stream of treats.

"He senses something," Karl said. I knew he was only sensing bribery, but I nodded just the same.

"Do you ever think about the resurrection, Karl?"

"Nope. Only two places you can go, heaven or purgatory."

"Oh, you don't believe in hell?"

"Oh yeah, there's hell, but I have been instructed that purgatory is kind of like this life here."

"Well, the Bible doesn't say anything about purgatory, but it says a lot about our resurrection as well as heaven and hell." *There shall be no more thence an infant of days* (Isaiah 65:20). "Do you have a Bible?"

"I've been instructed that man interprets the Bible to suit himself. I have one over there," he pointed to an overflowing table against the wall. It might as well have been across the parking lot. All I saw was his massive photo album. *Nothing could survive under that*, I thought.

"I don't see a Bible, but I see the photo album you showed me with all the pictures of your family. You're a self-made man, Karl, why would you let somebody tell you what to think? Why wouldn't you take it up and read the Bible for yourself?"

"I made a million dollars. I know because the accountant I had back then showed me. I told my kids, 'Don't say anything against your mother, or I'll take away the money.' That's what I did, too."

So much for the comfort found in his remaining eight children. I knew I had made no impact. My words did no more than pepper the pride of this old man like the little rolled up spitballs we used to make in grade school, bouncing off him and landing lightly on the twisted green snake on the floor. I stepped over the clutter as I stood to go, patting Karl on the knee.

"I don't want to get too much into your personal business, Karl. Levi and I just wanted to pay you an Easter visit. It was good to see you again."

While Karl had his sad Saturday agenda of death ...*a rebellious people... Which remain among the graves* (Isaiah 65:2,4), Levi and I were scheduled for a program of Life at an inner-city nursing home. They don't prefer my music visits, so I offered a hymn sing with Scripture and prayer. I didn't especially want to venture out on Saturday morning, but between my budget and my calling, I was constrained to go.

After dragging Levi's stroller up the outside steps (no ramp) and passing through the double-locked doors, we greeted our morning friends. Many were not mentally well, and a few looked like they'd narrowly escaped homelessness. I often wonder how close I might have come to calling a place like this my home, and I'm reminded to be thankful. It's a tough crowd, but with Christ, it's a welcomed opportunity.

The program title was "Easter, Death and Life!" I had emailed it ahead of time to the activities director, so printed copies were lying on a table ready to be passed out around the small dining room.

Our subject matter proclaimed that Jesus' resurrection procures and promises our own. Ten minutes in, a surprisingly well-dressed man in the corner raised his hand.

"I don't care about the resurrection, it's spiritual. I'm born again, and that's the resurrection, that's all that matters to me."

"Wait a minute," I replied, using my best cake-in-the-oven analogy. "You're not 'done' yet. Our bodily resurrection is the goal of our salvation! Yes, you could say being born again is the first resurrection, but God will raise up these same bodies"—patting my legs— "from the dust when Christ comes again. There's a new body coming for God's people and Christ died and rose to give you that!" I turned to the group, and heads were nodding, confirming that most of us were already groaning and ready for such a redemption. Everyone but this well-dressed man, apparently, who crossed his arms and was silent. *If in this life only we have hope in Christ, we are of all men most miserable* (I Corinthians 15:19).

To break the mood I asked for hymn requests, and a woman younger than I raised her hand.

"Were You There When They Crucified My Lord?"

"Oh, wonderful, I love that hymn and it's perfectly appropriate for Easter weekend. What's your name?"

"Emendisvere. People call me 'Em'."

Now, if you'd ever heard that name before, you would not forget it, and I am among the great minority who has. I had heard it once before.

Pausing the program, I said, "I hope you don't mind my asking, is your mother living?"

"No."

"Oh, I am sorry. Was her name Victoria?"

"Yes."

Pausing again, "Everyone, will you please excuse me just for a minute? I want to say something privately to Em over there, it will just take a moment, and I'll be right back. Just one minute, thanks."

Turning off my headset mic and pulling Levi along with me, I approached her. "Levi and I visited your mother all the time in the nursing home up the street. I was with her about two days before she died."

A shadow of emotion flickered across her face. "Oh... I saw her two weeks before. I couldn't go again, I was in the hospital." She thought for a moment. "Did my mother say anything?"

"No, my last visit was very close to her death, and she couldn't speak. But I sang hymns to her, I talked to her, I reminded her of what I knew about her. She moved her eyebrows and her eyes and hands twitched a little bit, I had the sense that she could hear me. I was there a long time. I really liked your mother; she was very sweet."

She nodded, "Yes she was."

Our program continued with no more interruptions, and disappointingly, not much participation. But asking for prayer requests brought a flurry of hands springing up across the dining room.

"Pray for me, I have anxiety."

"Pray for me, I'm a Christian, I'm not supposed to be sad, but I have depression."

"Pray for my salvation."

"Pray that I'll be patient until I see my mother again." This from our new friend, Emendisvere.

Christ was with us that morning because He was welcomed there. No pride (except maybe from the arms-crossed-man) pushed Him away. No haughty looks despised his broken body or the nail prints in His hands. No self-made man refused to thrust his hand into Christ's open side, to handle Him and see that it was He Himself, offering incorruptible life and beauty from the blood and ashes of His death.

Not even the sudden loss of the dearest babe (or beast) is apart from the will of our Father (Matthew 10:29). The cruel grave, the barren nursing home, the lifelessness of our own minds or bodies will never keep our Savior from caring for His own. Our earthen vessels will return to the dust in dependence on Christ and be raised, or we will decay in the strength of our rebellion and be damned.

But who would be foolish enough to refuse such a resurrection as this?

For why will ye die,
O house of Israel?
For I have no pleasure in the death of him that dieth,
saith Lord GOD:
wherefore turn yourselves,
and live ye.
Ezekiel 18:31-32

40

Nice Things

A comedian once told the story of getting into trouble as a child because he broke a superhero jelly jar glass from his mother's kitchen cabinet. "I guess we just can't have nice things," she said.

Now, unless we believe prosperity preachers, most Christians know that our best blessings are spiritual in nature.

But what about temporal "nice things," like a faster computer, or God forbid, the used car of our dreams? Are we ever allowed to have them? If so, must we be careful to maintain a healthy dose of guilt so that we don't enjoy them too much?

I support a small budget. I have been known to cry over big expenditures, even when I have the money. It's a fearful thing for me to open my clenched fists and part with the big bucks. Especially if I'm spending it on something I really want.

And now you see my conflict.

Do I really want it? Then surely I shouldn't have it.

I don't know if this is a "faith-based illness" or my own personal neurosis. I have a feeling it's a combination of both.

I have owned many cars in my lifetime. With most of them I have enjoyed a close personal relationship, calling them all by name: Petey was first, followed by Libby, Phoebe, and Lilly, to mention a few. The only exception was the Kia that was broken into and ripped apart at two in the morning a foot away from my front steps. (The thugs meant to steal it but were confounded by the manual transmission.) I didn't love that car. The Lord had provided it when I was in a bind, and I was grateful. But that's as far as it went.

What I really wanted at the time was my dream car, a Mini Cooper Countryman. I had shopped, prayed, and most importantly, agonized night and day over the prospect. Wise counsel advised that a Mini would be expensive to maintain, so in the end, I shied away and bought the economical emergency Kia that was ravaged in my driveway. But the morning after the break-in it didn't look like such a bargain anymore. Turns out nine other vehicles of the same make and model as mine were violated that night. I knew I would never feel safe in that car again. I had to replace it.

Once my Kia was towed to the repair shop, the rental car company dispatched a courtesy driver in a Chevy Spark (the very economy model I'd requested) to pick me up.

As we drove, I babbled on to the nice driver about how perfectly fitting the Chevy was for me. It was small, a hatchback, easy for me to handle, etc. "Low is good," I stressed. "I always say you can't fall too far if you're already close to the ground."

Pulling into the rental lot, we parked in front of something very red, shiny, and full of chrome.

"Oh my goodness, can I have that?" I said, jumping out and pointing a shaking finger at a gleaming Mini Cooper Countryman. I didn't even think to be embarrassed after spouting off for five miles about the wisdom of hovering at ground level. I was ready to fly.

She was only five dollars more a day and still covered under my insurance. Other than the color (I preferred white or black) and the automatic transmission (I preferred a stick shift), she was a dream come true.

She was so accommodating, such a pleasurable combination of high breeding and mannerly conduct. She said things like, "Oh, yes, I see that nasty truck, would you like me to hop into that empty lane way over there on the left?" And no sooner said, than she'd whisked us to safety, flashing a fading glimpse of her shiny rear bumper at the rude eighteen-wheeler who was left choking on her dust.

And now you see my desire. Which can really interfere with hearing clearly from the Lord.

I shopped, prayed, and agonized all over again, caught between my resurfacing obsession and the accompanying conflict. But this time wise counsel was surprisingly encouraging. Suddenly everyone just wanted me to be happy. Neighbors, relatives, even strangers gave me words of comfort, agreeing that a Mini would be perfect for me. My mechanic said, "You'll be fine," and a dear brother in the Lord even prayed, "May the Lord give you a Mini Cooper!"

I found what seemed to be a beautiful option at a dealership far, far away. She was a black and white stick-shift Countryman from seven years ago with only 40,000 miles on her ticker. The Lord answered prayer and a couple from my church volunteered to drive me down and support me in my negotiations. I took advice from the husband's business acumen and with a masterful show of intimidation convinced the salesman to shave a thousand right off the top. My girlfriend was impressed. I was ready to buy.

The finance office gal kept us waiting for two hours during which time I could hardly stay awake. To compensate I pumped myself full of four free cappuccinos from the machine in the waiting room. We'd had no lunch. By the time she appeared I was still exhausted but wired to the max and becoming very queasy.

Shutting the door behind us, Ms. Finance went to her computer and began to research extended protection plans. Her eyes grew big as she looked nervously from her screen, to me, and back again.

"You must be buying a car that's very expensive to repair because these plans are quite costly! Let me see if there's *anything* I can possibly do...."

I hadn't considered a protection plan; I had never bought one before. But now the fear of replacing an engine or transmission began racing around my caffeinated brain with lightning speed. Warnings from the naysayers of the past rose up in chorus against me. I managed to say "No" to $5,000 over five years to cover every unforeseen disaster but barely made it into the ladies' room before falling to pieces.

I'd signed all the papers, the deed was done, and there was no backing out. By the time I got home I was violently ill and became totally dehydrated. Unable to finish a sentence, I called 911, thinking I was having a stroke.

The ambulance appeared at my curb in no time. Refusing the stretcher, I was assisted inside by three very sweet young male technicians. Just between us ladies, I hadn't anticipated an EKG and was not properly attired for such an intrusive procedure. The dear boys were as discreet as possible with me, and I was too ill to be more than mildly embarrassed. Thankfully, I passed the heart, sugar, and blood pressure tests.

"Well, you're not having a stroke, but you're dehydrated. We'd like to take you to the hospital," said one young man. I figured I could handle rehydration on my own, so I received permission to hobble back up the walk to my door, simultaneously offering my most heroic "queen's wave" to the neighbors who stood watching from their driveway.

A few dozen saltines and several bottles of electrolytes later, I began to come around. But I was still convinced I'd made the most expensive and disastrous decision of my life, and my stomach would not stop agreeing.

The next day I cautiously drove my new car to our nursing homes, praying I would soon relax and all would be well. I came home to find a puddle of oil in the driveway. In a fit I called the manager of the dealership.

"I'm bringing this back! I don't want it!" I shouted.

"You can't bring it back." (I was afraid of that.) "But bring it in and I'll fix it."

I canceled work and made the long return trip in a car that was leaking oil, expecting the engine to seize at every turn. Settling into my familiar position in the waiting room, I looked up to meet Ms. Finance introducing an unsuspecting client to the malicious coffee machine. She hailed me with an exaggerated hello.

"How ARE you?" she said through the teeth of a full-faced smile.

I felt quite guilty about my weak little nod, but it was the best I could do.

After an hour, the goodwill greeter and the service manager approached me in tandem, their faces locked in identical expressions. They looked me in the eye and sweetly explained, "There's a little plug that you have to replace every time you change the oil. We just didn't know. It's fine now."

And now you see my ignorance. I believed them.

A few days later I took my new machine to my mechanic for a double-check. I was feeling a bit better about my decision, but I still had no peace. I was hoping he'd give me a good word.

He put my car up on his lift and called me under, pointing up to the oil pan.

"There's no plug at all. They stripped the plug and put silicone on the hole to try to seal it shut. It's still leaking oil. I can't fix it.

The oil pan, gasket and filter have to be replaced. See, the filter is totally black. They never even changed the oil."

From underneath the car, I called the dealership manager. I reported what his men had done, along with the lies that they had fed me. I added that I had conveniently taken pictures of the hole and the blackened filter in case he would like to see them. I was quiet and calm and in complete control. He said he would be happy to pay for the repair. Of course he would. And suddenly, I had peace.

Yes, I am an ignorant woman who was the prey of a corrupt used car dealership. And in my foolishness I walked into that showroom with a sign on my forehead that read, "Easy mark, please cheat here." I was (at least emotionally) the victim of an underhanded finance woman whose desire was not to protect my purchase but to make as much money as possible on our transaction. As it turned out, all my negative guilt-producing feelings associated with that company were right on target. The proper response to hours spent with such despicable characters was to go home, become violently ill, and call 911.

But now you see my confidence.

I belong to a mighty God who cares for me, who sees what is done in secret, and says that anyone who touches me touches the apple of His eye (Zechariah 2:8).

My dear mechanic had my Mini repaired by the afternoon. He went over "Beatrix" with a fine-toothed comb, returning her to me with his approval.

"This is a good car. It's a lot better than your other one."

During our evening walk, Levi and I stopped to chat with a young neighbor who runs the local auto parts store. He hadn't heard, so I shared my saga. He was both surprised and sympathetic.

"So, what did you end up getting?" he asked.

"A used Mini Cooper Countryman," I said with a grin.

His face lit up. "I love those! That's the bigger one, their version of an SUV. I could see you in something like that. It suits you. I had a foreign car like that once," he recalled. "The parts are a little more expensive, you might spend just a bit more in repairs."

"Maybe so," I answered, shrugging my shoulders. "But do you know what? This is my dream car, probably a once-in-a-lifetime thing. Hopefully it'll last me a good long time."

Straightening up, I concluded, "I'm a Christian; I think the Lord gave this to me. I'll just enjoy it for as long as I can."

His eye is on the sparrow,
and I know He watches me.
–Civilla D. Martin, 1905

41

Truth

It wasn't my birthday. They weren't close friends. I wasn't really even invited. But I still had to go to the party.

I'm sure that Tommy, a long-ago neighbor, meant no harm when he called me out of the blue.

"Hey, Susan, it's your old pal Tommy. Listen, I just got a call from our friend Jack. He's hosting a birthday dinner for his sister on Saturday night. Everybody's going. The restaurant is right around the corner from where you live now. Are you coming?"

"Oh...am I invited?" It seemed a worthy question.

"Well, Jack didn't exactly say...but when I offered to call you he said to let him know if you're available and he'll change the reservation number." My big hint that I was not on the original guest list.

Now, thanks to Tommy's intervention, Jack had been put on the spot. He couldn't come right out and say I wasn't invited. And I was on the same spot. If I declined to attend, that would only make things worse. So I accepted.

A few minutes later, Tommy called back to say Jack had "invited us" to pay our own way. I cannot tell you how much this added to the warm and fuzzy feelings already stewing in my breast. Nevertheless, come Saturday night, my ol' pal Tommy picked me up and drove us to the happy-birthday dinner.

Although I hadn't seen them in ages, I still cared for these people. But I also remembered they are not a sensitive bunch. Jack once tossed off a story of his father grabbing his mother's cat by the tail and slinging it across the highway after it had messed in their new car. And Jack was laughing.

Anyway, as I said, I care for them and was glad enough to see them. The first half of the meal went surprisingly well. Then the predictable occurred: Right in front of everyone, I disappeared.

Conversations had settled into little pockets, and I had already shared my one interesting story. I felt myself sinking into obscurity, the familiar brown paper bag closing over my head, its little smile etched in crayon and the words "never mind" scrawled across the top. As always, I grew weary of trying to push myself in, of working so hard to be included. Despite the years, nothing had changed.

But I still had to "pay my own way."

Tommy deals in cash and carries a hefty wallet. I do not. So we'd agreed ahead of time that I would pay with my credit card, and he would reimburse me.

Everyone was standing to go as I frantically tried to figure the tip using the calculator on my phone. I wanted to make our bill an even fifty dollars so that Tommy and I could easily divide it on the way home. The waitress returned my card just in time for me to follow the group out to our cars.

From beneath my paper bag, I watched Jack and Tommy in their lively closing conversation, feeling excluded and sorry for myself.

In the car I explained to Tommy that he owed me thirty dollars, as his dinner had cost more than mine. This included his share of the tip.

"You're very free with my money," he said, referencing my overwhelming generosity to the waitress. He reluctantly handed me the cash, and I was glad to take it. By then I thought I'd earned it.

Coming into my little house, I angrily ripped off the paper bag and prayed for peace to return. But in my time-honored tradition, weeping and processing must last at least for the night.

The next morning, instead of heading to Sunday school, I found myself where my serious processing always occurs: on the porch with my Bible, Levi, and coffee.

In the presence of the Lord, I tried to understand my disappearing act. My personality is generally not the "never mind" type. I am almost always noticeable; you can ask anyone. So why could I never be myself with this group?

The Reformed tradition is very good about teaching confession to the Lord, so in compliance I asked the Lord to show me my sin. I expected Him to reveal a problem in my thoughts towards the birthday bunch or in my conduct towards them. Instead, I was led into a study of the sanctity of Truth.

Let's consider the first sin.

[T]he woman being deceived was in the transgression (I Timothy 2:14).

It's a sin to tell a lie. But it's also a sin to let yourself believe one.

What was happening when that paper bag came over my head, when I sank into self-pity, shut down, and came home crying? I was sinning, that's what was happening. I was letting myself be deceived, and that was my transgression. I believed that what the birthday bunch thought about me was true. Their time-honored tradition is to devalue, overlook, and dismiss me. But God says I'm valuable–worth dying for, for heaven's sake. God says I'm so visible that He's had His eye on me from all eternity past. In fact, if you want to be very bold about it, I was the only one at the table (at least so far as I can tell) who could be called the temple of the living God. Yes, I was the "odd man out," but that bag did not belong upon my head. I wear a crown.

Job is famous for retaining his integrity in the face of his accusing "friends," and in that, he did not sin. *God forbid (or literally, pollution to me) that I should justify you: till I die I will not remove mine integrity from me* (Job 27:5). In other words, Job would have been contaminated–incurred his own guilt–if he'd believed his friends. Just because someone says something about you, it doesn't mean it's true.

And think of Daniel. If I'd been tossed into the lion's den, I would have thrown myself down in shame, convinced that I must have deserved such punishment. I'd have mentally strewn myself all over the cave before the beasts even opened their mouths. But Daniel maintained his innocence. He believed God, not the lions.

[F]orasmuch as before him innocency was found in me; and also before thee, O king, have I done no hurt...and no manner of hurt was found upon him, because he believed in his God (Daniel 6:22b, 23b).

Along with Daniel, I have learned to interpret dreams, predictable as mine might be. Nocturnal threats to my car, dog, or guitar usually indicate my own insecurity. The night of the disastrous birthday bash I dreamed that someone wanted to buy my beautiful Mini Cooper. But I did not want to sell it.

On my back porch the next morning, I was reminded of the verse *Buy the truth and sell it not* (Proverbs 23:23). To "buy" means to own. To "sell" means to surrender. (My dream car belongs to me, baby, I own it and I'm not giving it up.) Job and Daniel held onto the Truth. They owned it, would not surrender it, and this is to their praise and the glory of God.

My therapist once told me that if it were up to him, I would stay angry for the rest of my life for what happened to me in my childhood. Psychology tells us that anger defends us from depression, and I can see that, to a point. But anger is not the real defender. Truth is the Grand Protector, the Sword and Shield of our spirits.

Anger is a prison. Truth will stop the tears of ancient traumas, Truth will grow us up, and Truth will set us free.

In the end, the birthday-dinner incident had an ironic conclusion. The fifty dollars I paid for our meal never showed up on my credit card bill. After a month I called the card company. They confirmed that no charge had been registered, so I called the restaurant. The manager was very sweet.

"I appreciate you calling. I'm in the kitchen; let me see if my phone can reach the computer. What were the last four digits of your card? Yes, I see the fifty-dollar transaction; it says it went through last month. I think we're okay, honey."

Somehow, in God's kindness, my criminally clever credit card had managed to pay the restaurant without letting the card company know what it was up to.

I confess to you that my own criminal inclination was to keep back Tommy's thirty dollars as a consolation prize from the Lord. You'll be proud to know that I repented and returned it by check. Sanctification is an ongoing process, and it's apparent that I remain a work-in-progress.

But at least I didn't have to buy my own dinner.

Believe in the LORD your God,
so shall ye be established;
believe his prophets,
so shall ye prosper.
II Chronicles 20:20

42

People Get Ready

Even though my work is my ministry, it's important to keep up my guard. The problem is, I forget to do it.

Peeking into a room in one of my favorite facilities, I met the gaze of a man with a handsome haircut and tortoise shell glasses. He was perched up high in his bed beside a Yamaha keyboard that nearly spanned its length. I was about to knock when Hannah, a younger, very tall and heavy-set woman pushing a too-low walker with her fingertips approached me.

"Oh, is that Levi?"

"Yes it is!"

"Oh, will you come back to my room with me so I can sit on my bed and you can sing to me? It's right across the hall." It's wonderful to be wanted.

The conversation opened like a flower to the things of God, as easy and unscripted as could be. I sang "Just As I Am" while looking down into Hannah's gentle, open face. She was settled on the edge of her bed, her jaw relaxed, her eyes fixed on me.

> *Just as I am, without one plea,*
> *But that thy blood was shed for me,*
> *And that thou bidst me come to Thee,*
> *Oh Lamb of God, I come, I come.*
> –Charlotte Elliot, 1835

"You have a beautiful voice, so soft and pretty."

"Oh, thank the Lord Jesus. He took me out of the bars where I used to sing, and I'm sober over twenty years now."

Then Hannah shared of her own addiction and the sobriety resulting from her three years of nursing home life. "I can't drink when I'm in here."

"Do you remember that hymn?" I asked. "Billy Graham used it in his crusades. The choir would sing it when people would come down the aisle to pray to receive the Lord. I used to make fun of Billy Graham before I came to Christ. But now I love that hymn, because it talks about the way we come to God. I'm empty-handed, I got nothin'." I stretched out my open palms. "He's got everything."

She smiled. "I like that. Thank you for that." *Blessed are the poor in spirit, for theirs is the kingdom of heaven* (Matthew 5:3).

Positively glowing, I left her room with the very fragrance of Christ wafting about me. Next on the list of my own crusade was the smart-looking musician across the hall.

"Hi, knock-knock, I work here, may I come in?" I wheeled Levi up to him. "What's your name?"

"Frank."

"Oh, hi Frank, I'm Susan and this is L—"

"Sinatra." His monotone dripped with sarcasm. A funny guy.

I pretended to appreciate his humor. "Hah, that's funny, 'Frank,' I see your keyboard. Are you a musician?"

"Yeah, jazz."

Of course it was jazz. After putting me in my place by withholding his real name, he now was dwarfing my little folkie-self with his superior form of musicianship. But however low I may go, I persevere because I am very stubborn and this is my job.

"That's a beautiful picture on your keyboard, is that your wife? Your wedding day?"

"What date is today? It's the fourteenth, right? This is the anniversary of her death. I got the call at work, 'Your wife passed out in the grocery store,' and that was the beginning of the end. Fifty-nine days later she was gone. Left me with two kids, thirteen and fifteen."

"Frank, I am so sorry, I know how hard anniversaries like this can be."

He went on and on and on. I began to feel I'd stumbled into a tunnel that had no light at the end, just the stench and heat of a screeching train bearing down on my heels as I raced to make it out alive. It didn't look good for me.

I tried to fast forward his life to a better place. "How old are your children now?"

He searched the ceiling. "Thirty-six and thirty-eight."

"And how are they doing?" Never ask a question unless you know the answer, the lawyers say.

"They never got over it. We had cancer counseling, grief counseling, it didn't do any good." So, everyone's lives were ruined and remain ruined beyond repair to this very day.

"Have you ever found any comfort from the Lord?" (Never ask a question....)

"That Methodist minister came to our house and said, 'All things are possible with God.' My little daughter went nose-to-nose with him and said, 'Then don't let my mommy die!'"

"Frank, I am so sorry if that minister led you to think that God heals everyone. God never said He would do that. I'm so sorry, but we know that people die. God did say He's conquered death and He offers His children hope and eternal life and a glorious future."

I continued to make no visible impact on Mister Sinatra. But I am very stubborn and this is my job.

"May I sing something for you before I go?" (Emphasis on *going*.)

"Knock yourself out." It's wonderful to be wanted.

I sang, I left, saving Levi as through the fire, with the sting of it in my nostrils and the smell of smoke on my clothes. The train may have missed me, but I was not unscathed. ...*Neither cast ye your pearls before swine, lest they trample them under their feet, and turn again and rend you* (Matthew 7:6).

"Frank" was my last morning visit. Coming into the office for my coat, I met my Christian boss, a lovely woman who always speaks openly of Christ. I let loose.

"I was blind-sided! You know I want to be sympathetic, I want to hear people's stories, but this man is a bottomless pit of despair! He's in there feeding his misery with a spoon and happy to do it for the rest of his life."

"That's ministry." She took a deep breath, shook her body slightly and swept down her sides with her hands. "The important thing is not to wear it."

I didn't know what she meant. I thought she meant I shouldn't let it show, and I quickly qualified that "Frank" hadn't seen my frustration. But she explained, "Don't let it cling to you."

I don't usually think in those terms, but I could see her point. Being a sponge by nature, I do not excel at letting things go. I guess I felt so overwhelmed because I have a few of "Frank's" tendencies in my own heart. Everything bothers me. It's only by the grace of God that I don't sit in my own room day after day, rehearsing every sorrow and shaking my fist at heaven.

It is always, and only, by the grace of God.

My afternoon visits begin with Natalie and José. She is bed bound and sharp as a tack. He is very dear, mobile, and showing signs of memory loss and dementia.

Natalie often brings up the subject of God, challenging me on what I think. That's because "thinking" and "theories" are what matter to her.

"I don't believe in the God of the Old Testament. All that violence."

"You mean 'The Lord is my Shepherd, I shall not want?' 'The Lord God, merciful and gracious, longsuffering and abundant in goodness and truth?'" I can counter until I'm blue in the face. José stands beside me, hands folded in front, nodding along with everything I say. ...*except ye be converted and become as little children, ye shall not enter into the kingdom of heaven* (Matthew 18:3).

Unperturbed, Natalie continues, "Did you watch those documentaries at Christmastime? The ones that showed where the star really came from and said that Jesus was probably married?" *Ever learning, and never able to come to the knowledge of the truth* (II Timothy 3:7). It's all I can do to present a calm demeanor, exit quietly, and not race out of the room, barely inches ahead of the fire-breathing train once again.

On the second floor, Paul is stretched out in the longest bed available in skilled care, all six feet seven inches of him. A former musician and singer, he damaged his hearing with years of loud performing and can only hear me because of my little headset and speaker.

"Susan, I can't get over Christmas. There was nothing. Nobody came, nobody. My family has money. But everything I own is in that cupboard over there." He turns to me. "I wish I had a friend." I wish he did, too.

"Paul, don't forget, you and I will be together *forever*."

"That's right, we're brother and sister in the Lord." He smiles and we fist bump solidly to consummate our eternal relationship. "You know what I want to hear. I'll sing as much as I know."

I come to the garden alone, while the dew is still on the roses—

Raising his hands to heaven, Paul cries out, "Hallelujah! Lord Jesus, pour your Holy Spirit down on me!"

I want to ride on Paul's train, the one that's bound for glory. I want to sit next to Hannah, with my pockets empty and my open palms outstretched. I know my Lord will save me from that long, black train that comes screaming without warning and steals away souls in the night. I have felt its hot breath and smelled its smoke. I have been moments away from being flattened beneath its rage, my remains drawn headlong into the vacuum of that lightless eternal night. My heels are charred and my lungs are black but see, I am comely and my soul is white and clean within me.

So we ride together—Paul, Hannah, and José too, along with all the other blind, lame, and poor who have had the gospel preached to us. Perched up high and on the right side of the rails, we are being swept securely along towards the glorious end of the children of God. We search and search among ourselves, but not one of us seems to hold a ticket. We don't know how we got here.

We just thank the Lord.

Parting Thoughts

Dear Friend,

Although we haven't met, it has meant the world to me to share my story with you. Thank you for coming alongside and listening so patiently. Even though our lives are so different, it wouldn't surprise me to learn that we have much in common—maybe not in our circumstances, but in our hearts.

I often wonder what would have happened to me if God hadn't intervened in my life, uncalled for and undesired, over twenty years ago. I wonder if I'd even be alive. Would I have been killed by liver disease, drugs, or someone's irate wife? Or succumbed to despair like my father? Maybe I'd still be dressing like a teenager and singing in a bar somewhere. Or homeless and living in a cardboard box. Would I have a friend in the world?

I wanted success. I chased fame, I drank and had affairs, and all these idols made me feel better, for the moment, about myself. But God took the alcohol, He took the sex, He never let me have the fame, and when He made me His own, He sent me into nursing homes to serve the elderly and ill who live there. He came against me, and He turned me around. Who would I be now if He hadn't?

There's a Scripture in the old King James that reads, *no feller comes against us* (Isaiah 14:8). The first time I read it I laughed out loud, because it sounded like a hillbilly sayin' "feller" instead of "fellow." Of course it's the trees that are speaking, meaning no one comes with an ax to "fell" them. But you and I are not trees. We are people who desperately need God's ax. It's when we are left to ourselves that we fall to ruin.

For whom the Lord loves He chastens, God says, in Hebrews 12:6. This is the comfort of the sons of God. To be left as we are is to make us illegitimate children who will fester in our filth until our sins pile up to heaven. To be given up by God is the greatest terror known to man. But God's own people, who fear this terror, will never face it, because He who comes against us is for us. His name is Emmanuel, God with us.

As I write these parting thoughts to you it is Christmastime. I still struggle with sadness at this time of year. It can be a difficult season for many; maybe you feel it, too.

But if you have some time, search the internet for the Christmas day scene of the different versions of *A Christmas Carol* and watch them all in a row. Dickens never says outright that Ebenezer was born again, but witness a dead man coming to life, again and again. Rejoice with our new friend as he laughs and bellows, dances like a fool, jumps for joy, and compliments the "fine fellow" he sends to buy the biggest turkey in the butcher's window. "What an intelligent boy!" To those who know the Lord, this can only be His doing, and it is marvelous in our eyes.

I leave you in the hope that we will always remember to pray for the desperate and lonely people of this world, even as we pray for ourselves. We, who have been blessed to have our lives broken into and turned upside down by the King who still reaches up from the manger. For nothing shall be impossible with God.

Your friend in Christ,
Susan

Acknowledgments

Oh, my dearest nursing home friends, may the Lord one day show you the many lives you have blessed and the power you possess. In your weakness and transparency, you change the world.

Dr. Richard Ievoli, you told me that one day I would write you an epic. Saving my life was not enough for you; you had to predict the future, too. I will always love you.

I am eternally grateful to you, Pastor Bruce Sofia, for boldly speaking the Words of Life used by God to set me free. (I'm also relieved that any similarity between you and you-know-who turned out to be nothing more than a nice suit and well-trimmed beard.)

My loving appreciation goes to pastors Fred Pugh, Marty Murtha, Dabney Olguin, and the elders and deacons of Grace Covenant Church. You not only taught me of Christ, fed me in Word and groceries, pulled up my shrubs, and laid down my kitchen tile, but you prayed me through this process. You are men to be trusted.

Heartfelt thanks to my God-given editor Nancy Sayre for your undying patience and invaluable direction during the endless rewrites of a first-time author. Your skill at untangling my cryptic storytelling made this book comprehensible for more than maybe just one person.

All the gratitude that the limits of human adoration can bear belongs to my first canine ministry partner, Chloe. You sweet, funny girl, I will cry for you until the day I die. And although you never got to meet him (he would have driven you crazy), your little pip-of-a brother Levi has managed to fill up my poor heart once again. Little boy, what would I do without the love and joy you bring to us all?

About the Author

Guitar in hand, 15-year-old Susan Piper walked into the Cleveland bars in pursuit of stardom. A couple of decades later, Jesus decided that was long enough and pulled her out again with His mighty outstretched arm.

During those wine-soaked years, Susan won the Kerrville Texas Songwriting Competition; performed in a multitude of dives and even some nice venues, including the Philadelphia Folk Festival; and recorded two albums for Sliced Bread Records. Since her conversion to Christ, she only sings in lovely places and has recorded seven CDs about her Savior.

The Lord again showed His mighty hand during a sudden illness, gifting her with a new love of writing prose. The illness didn't last, but the writing did.

Nowadays, guitar in hand, Susan walks into nursing home rooms with her canine partner, Levi. When she's not working, Susan enjoys as much excitement as a highly sensitive person can stand in her little town in Northeast Ohio. Her pastimes include writing, solving British crime dramas, and pedaling Levi around in his bicycle basket. *A Blessing Is in It* is Susan's first book.

Listen to Susan's music at www.susanpiper.com. Write to her at susan.piper@onekingpress.com.

www.ingramcontent.com/pod-product-compliance
Lightning Source LLC
LaVergne TN
LVHW041921070526
838199LV00051BA/2687